TAI

.ear
LS

r bet
ıl if

. tʰ

ıl a
inᶜ

Risk management in civil, mechanical and structural engineering

Health and Safety Executive
Institution of Civil Engineers

Risk management in civil, mechanical and structural engineering

Proceedings of the conference organized by the
Health and Safety Executive in co-operation with
the Institution of Civil Engineers, and held in
London on 22 February 1995

Edited by M. James

 Thomas Telford

Published by Thomas Telford Publishing, Thomas Telford Services Ltd, 1 Heron Quay, London E14 4JD

First published 1996

Distributors for Thomas Telford books are
USA: American Society of Civil Engineers, Publications Sales Department, 345 East 47th Street, New York, NY 10017-2398
Japan: Maruzen Co. Ltd, Book Department, 3–10 Nihonbashi 2-chome, Chuo-ku, Tokyo 103
Australia: DA Books and Journals, 648 Whitehorse Road, Mitcham 3132, Victoria

A catalogue record for this book is available from the British Library

Classification
Availability: Unrestricted
Content: Collected papers
Status: Authors' opinion
User: Civil, Mechanical and Structural Engineers, Construction Managers

ISBN: 0 7277 2063 5

Printed and bound in Great Britain by Redwood Books, Trowbridge, Wiltshire.

Synopses of papers

Design developments. *P. A. Merriman*
The effect on the design process of safety standards are reviewed through case studies of the Thermal Oxide Reprocessing Plant (THORP) Cumbria. The development of design criteria, and experimental work associated with extreme hazards are summarised. Examples are given of the construction details adopted to reduce the consequences to acceptable levels. The general lessons for future projects are highlighted.

Risk analysis for the Channel Tunnel. *D. Parkes and C. Milloy*
The planning for the Channel Tunnel had to deal with tunnel construction hazards compounded by logistical problems of working up to 22 kilometres out beneath the sea. In order to satisfy the concerns of the Health and Safety Executive and to provide a rational basis for the design of safe plant and operating procedures, probabilistic techniques were used to supplement an intimate knowledge of tunnelling operations.

Risk-based decision-making in bridge maintenance. *N. C. Knowles*
This paper focuses on the use of formal decision-making methodologies to balance the sometimes competing interests of safety, direct cost, environment and socio-political factors encountered in managing existing bridges. It is illustrated by reference to recent work in maintaining a major motorway bridge structure.

Process re-engineering for safety. *D. Blockley*
Technical and organisational learning from lessons drawn through the management of hazard is emphasised. Hazard is defined as a set of preconditions to failure which can be managed directly. Risk can be managed only indirectly. A general framework for an approach which has information technology as a central resource in the re-engineering of technical and business processes is outlined.

A methodology for risk management in civil, mechanical and structural engineering.
M. J. Baker, R. J. Graves and M. Kearney
This paper represents a practical methodology for assessing and managing risk in the construction industry. This consists of a number of formal steps which are required to be carried out in sequence: hazard identification; investigation of possible triggering events; estimation of the likelihood and consequences of undesirable occurrences; and the selection of control measures to reduce the risks to acceptable levels. The paper gives details of the procedures required, and discusses the result from the desk studies and initial field trials.

Methods that apply to QRA in the construction industry. *J. Mather, C. D. Emery and P. Fewtrell*

This paper describes a current project being carried out by W. S. Atkins for the Health and Safety Executive to investigate methods that apply to Quantified Risk Assessment techniques in the construction industry. The work involves the development of a methodology to quantify risks at the design stage. The paper describes the approach adopted and discusses the collation of data by HSE Field Inspectors to quantify the matrix.

Factors affecting safety, cost and quality of scaffolding. *M. James*

This paper examines how the safety, cost and quality of a scaffold structure are affected by the relationship of the design to the abilities of the supervisors and workers, and how this relationship can be analysed by consideration of the components in the structure at varying levels of detail. This information is considered in dealing with risk management over the whole life of the scaffold: i.e. its manufacture, erection, use, dismantling cycles, storage and final scrapping.

Applying innovation to minimise financial and safety risks. *K. Ridgway, A. Todd and A. J. Wilday*

This author believes that designers should concentrate their efforts on the basic analysis of a system or product, and apply innovation to minimise financial and safety risks while maximising quality and cost benefits. The paper presents the outlines of this research, to investigate design methods and techniques for identifying the opportunity for innovation, discussion, traditional design methodologies and introducing the applicability of techniques such as value analysis to identify areas where innovation is required.

Life cycle cost management: a client's view. *K. Owen*

This paper describes BAA's Life Cycle Management philosophy in the analysis of projects, with both existing and alternative options being fully explored. The system adopted by BAA involves the development, design, procurement, construction, operation and maintenance of all BAA's facilities (assets) groupwide. The life cycle cost of an asset is defined as the total cost of the asset over its operating life, including initial acquisition costs and subsequent revenue (running costs), and the costs of disposal.

Contents

Chairman's Introduction

E HAMBLY   President of The Institution of Civil Engineers

Sadly, Edmund Hambly died soon after this conference took place. His opening remarks were recorded and are reproduced below.

Good Morning Ladies and Gentlemen. Firstly I am delighted to welcome you all here on behalf of both the organisers of the conference and the Institution. I am Edmund Hambly and will be the chairman for all of today. I've been asked to say a few words of introduction by Malcolm James of the HSE and I hope they set the conference off in the direction that he, as a prime mover of the conference, is hoping.

Anyway, my understanding is that this conference is to be productive, it is to help the HSE produce a booklet of guidance for all of us. Therefore, it is very important that we have a constructive debate about how we find our way forwards with the problems of trying to make risk management a productive rather than backward-looking exercise. Malcolm has coined the term Engineering Consequence Design. In other words, a process in which we look forward at every stage in the design to the problems of construction, operation, maintenance and removal of the facilities that we are designing.

There is nothing new about this, the best designers are already doing it. The booklet will actually make it a straightforward process, for every designer. So, when they start on a project, as they are starting to think of the function of a facility, they are also thinking of how it's going to be built, how it is going to be operated and so on. What we are talking about has to come in at the concept stage and I see three fundamental stages in this.

First we must have a clear understanding of the works we are designing or building. This is where the CDM regulations are to be commended : they say a safety plan must start off with a clear description of the project.

Then one has to have a visualisation of the hazards and we wanted to develop a technique that allows us to anticipate the hazards as we go along. If you imagine a desk to be some piece of a large building or an industrial facility then at the initial stage, when we visualise the layout of the plant, we visualise the hazards associated with it. So, if this is a roof overhanging, what are the problems of access underneath the lips ? and so on. Hence we immediately look at projects not just from a functional point of view but also from a safety point of view.

Finally, having visualised the hazards, how do we map them in our minds and on our drawings, so that we can, throughout the design process, design the hazards out of it ?

We can approach this in several ways. In the United Kingdom we tend to work towards providing a safe place of work, with scaffolding and so on. But this involves risks while providing the scaffold and later while using it. In the United States they go in much more for working safely and one might use steeplejacks working safely to achieve the same end.

I think an essential part of what we must do today is to keep our objectives simple and what we are trying to do simple. It is too easy to get bogged down in jargon and just wordage.

Now, risk assessment has many different definitions and some of them are tautologies. I noticed in an HSE document on rationalising risk assessment that the definition of risk assessment, given in the management of health and safety regulations, is to identify the measures needed to comply with the statutory requirements. In other words, risk assessment is to satisfy the statutory requirements for risk assessment !

Our objectives are rather more fundamental. We are trying to make the whole facility safer. Risk statistics, which we tend to get bogged down in, are very useful for highlighting areas where have we had problems in the past - falling objects, falling people and so on. I see them as an essential part of risk assessment but I am very sceptical about the predictive abilities of risk assessment. I think that, like weather forecasting, predicting precisely where human error is going to come in is extremely difficult. I know Malcolm would like to control safety completely and I like to pull his leg and that he must make some allowance for acts of God.

The problem is that we live in a chaotic world and chaos theory applies to predicting risks, just as it does to predicting weather. Therefore, we shouldn't go overboard in trying to be too analytical. I think that many of the risk assessments of a generation ago will be completely re-evaluated, in the light of the developments in weather forecasting and chaos theory.

However, to return to our subject today we have to be pragmatic and adopt a simple approach. We are aiming to find a way of providing guidance to engineers generally and a philosophy of design that takes full account of hazards as we identify them.

Keynote Address

Dr A F ELLIS, HSE : Director Technology & Health Sciences Division

There are two reasons why I am very pleased to be able to give this key note address. The first is because the conference is jointly sponsored by HSE and the Institution and is therefore a good example of the strong liaison between the HSE and the professions. Secondly because it will deal with a subject that is becoming such an important topic for engineers in all kinds of disciplines.

However, in some ways the current significance being given to Risk Assessment and Risk Management may seem a little strange because engineers have been doing assessing and handling risk issues since the first stone was placed upon another. The person undertaking this must surely have made some evaluation of the likelihood of it falling off and its consequences.

Essentially the evaluation of risk comes from experience; to be able to do it effectively requires that you need information if this is available about the outcome of other similar operations; that is to have knowledge of similar or related past experiences. For example the first builder I have just mentioned would have appreciated the weight and instability of the stones he was using from moving them around and noticing how easily some of them could be made to roll over.

Great engineers have been those who have been able to learn major lessons from the minimum of experience and then have applied these lessons to a very great effect. Smeeton, Telford, Brunel, Stephenson, men who have rightly been honoured by the nation and by this Institution in particular, all carried out very effective forms of risk management. That is why their structures have been so successful and have lasted as long as they have.

The difference today is that society and regulators are demanding proof that appropriate standards of risk management are being used particularly given the pressure to cut costs.

Many people believe that legislation is driving the concept of Risk Assessment, particularly as typified by new safety regulations. It is true that legislation has in some cases formalised what has in the past been good practice. Also, the legislators frequently follow where informed public opinion leads. For years we have seen considerable concern in our newspapers about this incident or that. We have also seen the steady rise in civil claims for accidents. All this creates the background for more rigorous Risk Management and of course for change.

Despite this demand for change within society there is also a strong element within most of us that resists change. We tend to dislike and distrust change unless we are absolutely convinced of its necessity. Faced with change we seem to adopt one of other two options.

We can ignore it, pretend that it has not happened and that it will go away, OR we can embrace it and investigate all the benefits and opportunities that it might offer us both as a society and as professional engineers.

I think that this conference is for those who intend to adopt this second option, who not only recognise the necessity for changing the way we deal with risk but also recognise that there could be significant benefits in it.

HSE's general approach to occupational risk starts with the truism that there is no such thing as absolute safety; all activities whether at work or play, involve some degree of risk. However, the risks to one's health and safety at work should be properly controlled in a reasonable way, which will both allow for technological progress and give a due regard for cost. The Health and Safety at Work Act frequently uses the term 'so far as is reasonably practical'. This has as its heart the concept that there is a relationship between cost and the reduction of risk and therefore require risk to be 'as low as is reasonably practical' or ALARP.

I am sure that many of you will be familiar with the ALARP philosophy. Below these levels, an activity can take place provided the risks have been made as low as reasonably practicable. Here a cost benefit assessment is required either implicitly or explicitly to weigh the cost and need or otherwise of additional safety measures. The higher the risk the more proportionately that would be required to reduce it.

Where the risks are less significant, the less proportionately it is worth spending to reduce them and at the lower end of the zone, it may not be worth spending anything at all. Below this range the risks are regarded as being broadly acceptable, being fairly negligible in comparison with the risks in our normal everyday lives.

Most engineers will, I imagine, want a clear idea where their particular work falls. How can one decide on what is the appropriate safety level for any particular activity.

Ultimately, of course, that is the business of the courts, but HSE establishes its own views partly out of its experience and judgement, partly out of national and international discussions and agreements, and partly on independent advice from the various advisory committees that are in place. Consultation with all interested parties is widespread when any changes particularly in legislation or guidance are proposed.

In some areas of risk, quantitative assessment has developed, initially being attractive to the regulator but viewed with suspicion by industry. More recently however both have converged at least some way towards appreciating the value of quantification even where the figures have been obtained as a result of engineering judgement rather than as a consequence of exhaustive testing.

A good example of this is the HSE discussion document 'The Tolerability of Risk from Nuclear Power Stations' which was first published in 1988 and reprinted 4 years later.

This went much wider than considering just nuclear risks and laid the foundation for many of the principles I have already described, which could then be used in many other industries. It also suggested some of the numerical points on the ALARP diagram.
For instance it is now widely agreed that the risk of death of 1 in 1000 per annum is about the most that is ordinarily accepted for workers in the UK.

When considering members of the public, one is thinking about a group some of who are susceptible to the threat whatever it may be - heat, radiation, toxic gas - and generally do not have the information, training and choices that workers have. Therefore the levels of <u>workers</u> need to be lowered for the public and HSE proposed that a risk of 1 in 10^4 per annum to any member of the public is the maximum that should be tolerated from any large industrial plant in any industry. This risk equates to the average annual risk of dying in a traffic accident. These are risks that might be regarded as "just tolerable".

We can also consider levels of risk that might be thought of as <u>broadly acceptable</u> so that s long as precautions are maintained, it would not normally be reasonable to consider further improvements to standards if these involved a cost.

There is general agreement and this was confirmed in our consultations outside HSE, that a risk of about 1 in a million or 1 in 10^6 per annum is considered to be broadly acceptable - but not negligible. It is roughly the same as being electrocuted at home. It requires us to be careful but not radically to change our ordinarily behaviour.

While we (HSE) think that such values do help to define the limits of tolerable risk, there is clearly a very large gap between these and their relation to the nuts and bolts of engineering.

My own division within HSE is starting to give serious consideration to the development of a design method or philosophy intended to allow designers and planners clearly to evaluate the risks involved in such 'nuts and bolts'. We presently call this the ENGINEERING of the CONSEQUENCES of the DESIGN or ECD for short.

This is the first public announcement about this project which is also the background to this conference, as we wish to explore how it might fit with work already undertaken in the Risk Management field, illustrate how the work is progressing and discover what the professional engineer thinks about it all. We shall hear more about various aspects of this work during the day and particularly about some of the results of research already undertaken.

The principle idea behind ECD is that safety is not and should not be a built on extra. It is an aspect of good management in the same way as other aspects, such as proper financial control and delivering a product to time at the correct quality.

There have been cases where structures have received accolades for their aesthetic appearance or technological innovation but have been extraordinarily difficult for example to maintain. Such structures which do not include reasonable provisions for safety, are NOT successes, certainly not in the sense we would normally associate with the best that Stephenson, Brunel or Telford could achieve in their day and with their resources.

It has often been said in the past that 'bolting on safety' can result in significant increases in the cost of a project. This may well be so. It must surely make sense to consider safety at the same time as all the other aspects of good management with much more favourable cost implications and the potential, at least in some instances, of cost reductions.

Estimates have been made that the implementation of the CONSTRUCTION DESIGN AND MANAGEMENT REGULATIONS (CDM), with its requirement for risk assessments to be carried out, will save up to £580M per annum. This net estimated saving arises from the savings in the cost of accidents and their associated consequences.

ECD is intended to be a PRO-ACTIVE method whereby the designer or planner can in effect select the appropriate level of risk, in terms of safety, cost and/or quality, and use this to control the design or plan as it evolves, advising the client accordingly.

There is one other aspect of ECD that I should mention. Any pro-active design method must inevitably increase the design effort, even though this should be well compensated for in the build or use stages. ECD is to be developed so that those areas that really need attention can be quickly and simply identified, thus enabling the available resources to be concentrated where they will give the maximum effect. As the philosophy develops and becomes more easy to quantify, then no doubt the use of IT systems will reduce even further any additional design effort.

As I said at the beginning of this address we are at the start of a major change in the way many design, plan and build. Most professional engineers, perhaps all professional engineers, are already very heavily loaded with work, that is the way of things nowadays. Change may seem to be the last thing most of us want especially when we consider the extra time needed for re-training, the slow familiarisation with new ideas and the effort to get our minds out of one track and into another.

But it seems to me that there are major opportunities in this emerging new world of Risk Assessment, opportunities to make substantial reductions in the level of accidents, opportunities in ensuring that we can supply just the right product for the right job, opportunities of improving the competitive edge of our engineers in this country.

Therefore, Mr Chairman, I hope that this conference will make the beginning of new developments with the engineering professions both for the benefits and welfare of the workers in our industries and for the benefit of this country as a whole.

SESSION 1
Some examples of current practice : Three case studies

Design Developments

P A MERRIMAN, BNF plc

1 INTRODUCTION

Over the last few years, the nuclear industry has made considerable progress in formulating their methodology for risk management - the major concern being radiological release to the environment. In 1988 the Health and Safety Executive (HSE) outlined their approach in "The Tolerability of Risk from Nuclear Power Stations" [1] This established that the licensees should initially demonstrate that the level of risk for their proposed operations was not sufficiently large that they would not be allowed to continue - that the level of risk is tolerable. Then measures necessary to avert the risk must be taken until or unless the cost of these measures, whether in time or money, is grossly disproportionate to the risk which would be averted. Therefore, risk must be reduced to a level as low as reasonably practicable - the ALARP principle. In all cases a point will be reached where the risk is, or has been designed to be, so small that no further precautions are necessary.

The nuclear industry has to comply with the Nuclear Installation Act 1965 - a subsidiary to the Health and Safety at Work Act 1974 - which applies specific regulatory controls to nuclear plants. Under this act, no nuclear plant may be constructed or operated unless a license has been granted by HM Nuclear Installations Inspectorate (NII) - the Nuclear Safety Division of the HSE. Before a license is obtained, the licensee must submit a safety case and supporting documents for assessment by the NII. To ensure a constant and uniform approach across the nuclear industry, the NII produced "Safety Assessment Principles for Nuclear Plants" [2] This was a consolidation of earlier separate nuclear power stations[3] and chemical plants[4] For new and existing plant it provides a flexible framework within which the Regulatory Authority will assess the safety case.

The THORP (Thermal Oxide Reprocessing Plant) complex at Sellafield was designed and constructed by BNF plc to provide reprocessing facilities for spent nuclear fuel from around the world. The Receipt and Storage Facility was the first part completed in 1988 and provides for the receipt of fuel flasks, the emptying of the flasks and the storage of the fuel below water until ready for reprocessing. In Head End the fuel rods are mechanically handled and the fuel is extracted into liquid form. Finally the liquid fuel is reprocessed in Chemical Separation area.

(i) Containment Philosophy - the need to identify the key structural components in providing radiological shield protection to operators and the provision of containment barriers throughout the process.

(ii) The development of a Building and Civils Brief from the Hazards and Operability Studies carried out by the Safety Department and Plant Operators.

(iii) The Development of Design Criteria to meet the 'new' natural hazards and abnormal conditions.

(iv) The change that Quality Assurance has had on the Design Process.

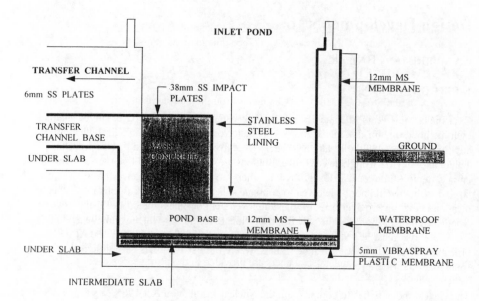

INLET POND SECTION

FIG 1

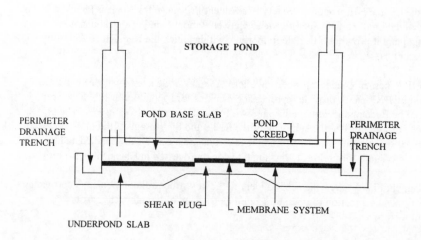

TYPICAL CROSS SECTION

FIG 2

Finally, in the summary the lessons that have been learnt from THORP which may be applicable to all projects will be discussed and recommendations given.

2. CONTAINMENT POLICY

In the Receipt and Storage Facility (5), the fuel is brought into the plant carried by rail. The fuel is removed from opened flasks in the inlet pond and then transported in containers to the Storage Ponds. There, the containers are positioned by the pond handling machine onto a supporting rack system. Storage below water is necessary to cool the fuel whilst the level of radioactivity reduces before further operations. The excess heat is removed by cycling the pond water through cooling towers.

In the inlet pond, during flask transport the flasks initially provide the shielding and heat rejection, and then the containers act as the primary containment Fig 1. Then the structural barrier and the secondary containment to water egress is the inner 3mm stainless steel liner. Therefore the inlet pond is not designed as a concrete water retaining structure. An alternative approach to stainless steel liners are provided in the Storage Ponds Fig 2. The main design objectives are that:

(i) the ponds should be designed to retain water and minimise leakage.

(ii) Any leakage should, as far as is reasonably practicable be detectable, collectable and quantifiable.

The concrete external walls, designed to water retaining codes, provide the barrier against leakage. All the walls are kept clear of attached services so that visual inspection is facilitated. These can be repaired during service by resin injection from the outside if necessary without emptying the pond. In the foundation, repairs are not practicable during service and there is the possibility of egress into the ground. Therefore a system of membranes is provided whose function is to reveal, and contain any leakage to collection sumps. This is illustrated in Fig 3. There are two membranes laid to slopes - an impervious polyurethane and a mild steel one to direct any leakage to collection trenches at the sides. During installation, all the membranes were tested by NDT means to ensure that any leakage through the walls would fall vertically and be contained in the trenches and recovered.

In the Head End and Chemical Separation Plants the main objectives are containment to ensure that both aerial and effluent releases are kept within acceptable limits and shielding to protect operators.

For the aerial releases, the key feature is the categorisation of the building into areas where different radiological activity levels may occur. The ventilation systems provide differential pressures, circulating the air from the lower active areas to the higher ones. This ensures that there is minimal risk to the environment and that operators work within controlled areas where the permitted radiation levels are unlikely to be exceeded. There is high reliability in the cascade ventilation system with designed diversity and redundancy. In the unlikely event of a breakdown, the concrete cells will provide the main containment. The outer cladding of the building, though less effective than the cells, will also provide supplementary containment.

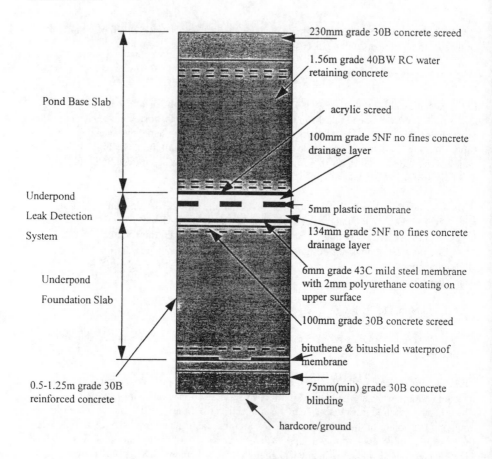

Pond Base Slab

Underpond

Leak Detection

System

Underpond

Foundation Slab

0.5-1.25m grade 30B
reinforced concrete

230mm grade 30B concrete screed

1.56m grade 40BW RC water
retaining concrete

acrylic screed

100mm grade 5NF no fines concrete
drainage layer

5mm plastic membrane

134mm grade 5NF no fines concrete
drainage layer

6mm grade 43C mild steel membrane
with 2mm polyurethane coating on
upper surface

100mm grade 30B concrete screed

bituthene & bitushield waterproof
membrane

75mm(min) grade 30B concrete
blinding

hardcore/ground

Pond Base and Membrane System

FIG. 3

In the Chemical Separation Building, the vessels and pipework act as the primary containment. The method of providing further barriers to reduce the risk of ground containment varies depending on the radioactive inventory of the plant. Where it is low, the thick concrete foundation slab is the effective second barrier. A 'decontaminable' steel liner is provided to ensure that, if a vessel or pipe leaks, the area can easily and quickly be cleaned up. Although in practice, the liner makes a significant contribution to the cells containment ability it is not considered a safety barrier. For higher inventories, bunds formed by qualified stainless steel liners are provided across the floors and up the walls. These are designed to ASME III - Div 2 standards which are constructed to be leak tight and therefore constitute the second barrier for containment. An additional safety feature is that the concrete foundation slab, as well as supporting the stainless steel cladding also minimises leakage into the ground.

The size of the majority of the concrete walls are determined by shielding requirements preventing the penetration of the ionising radiation. Where the thickness of the walls is reduced to accommodate plant items, barytes or lead concrete may be used to increase the effective shielding.

Overall the approach is to provide defence in depth to contain aerial and liquid release by providing multiple barriers for normal operating conditions. The building is split up into different radiological activity areas and the ventilation system draws air from low activity towards higher potential activity and final treatment before discharge (including monitoring). With shielding thicknesses, there is no redundancy so calculations are carried out to ensure the safety of the operator in a conservative manner.

3. DEVELOPMENT OF BUILDING & CIVILS BRIEF

Within BNF, the Safety Section are responsible, in conjunction with Plant Designers and Operators, for carrying out a Hazard and Operability Study (HAZOP) to identify and define safety and operability issues which may arise in the operation of the proposed plant. On large projects, the study team is composed of members from all the technical disciplines as well as experienced staff from the Operational and Monitoring Departments (Safety & Medical and Operational Health Physics Department) of the Sellafield site. There is a phased approach to the study. When the process or plant concept is produced a conceptual study is carried out HAZOP 1. Its major purpose is to subject the proposed design to its potential risks. The normal operations of the process or plant are examined to identify any significant hazards or operability problems associated with the design. At this stage, there is no requirement for supporting material to be prepared in detail.

The detailed study HAZOP II is initiated when firm sets of Engineering Flow Diagram/Engineering Line Diagrams and functional designs are available. The design is examined to identify where hazard and operability problems may occur from deviations from the normal plant status, and how they may be mitigated/eliminated to acceptable levels.

These studies will then form the basis for a Building and Civil Brief. These requirements have evolved over recent years to embrace three main conditions of loading:

(i) Normal Operating Loading which relates to plant, dead and imposed structural loads encountered in everyday operation. (Building Regulations).

(ii) Abnormal loadings which arise from the possible malfunction of plant and control equipment and are related to operations carried out within the THORP Plant.

(iii) Hazard loads which arise from the requirement that all natural hazards having a predicted frequency of being exceeded no more than once in 10,000 years should be designed for. Earthquake, temperature, snow, wind and flood hazards were all considered on the THORP project.

For these extreme conditions, it is only necessary for the plant to remain safe but not operational after the event. All components required for safety are classified as being safety related.

In addition, the radiological protection requirement for thickness of shielding and containment barriers are included.

To meet these briefs, design criteria were developed for the principal loading, both for the structural and liner components and experiments were carried out to confirm the behaviour under possible dropped impact of flasks. This work will now be described.

4. DESIGN CRITERIA FOR SAFETY RELATED STRUCTURES

4.1 Seismic Criteria

For earthquake resistance, the basis of design is that the structure conforms to specified performance criteria for the combined effects of the earthquake together with other loads present when the earthquake occurs. To ensure economic design, it was necessary to identify various grades of performance with associated stress levels that would meet the safety case. For the liquid containment barriers, the limiting condition is conservatively assumed to be when the concrete structure or liner departs from elastic behaviour. The aim is to ensure complete recovery of the structure after the earthquake and retention of its liquid retaining capability. The allowable stress levels were kept below yield - lower stresses being taken for the unlined containment structure Cat 1A - compared with the one incorporating a ductile liner, Cat 1B.

Another performance criterion identified was the possible requirement to maintain the precise alignment of plant so that materials etc can be recovered after the event. This would require not only substantial recovery but also control of deflections to avoid damage to plant and services, Cat 2. For concrete structures, allowable stresses were below those for 1B but greater than 1A.

Outside the concrete cell, it was acceptable that cracks and hinges could form in the structural members without affecting the radiological releases. The earthquake load is resisted by the capacity of the structure to absorb energy and, provided this capacity is not exceeded, transient mechanisms can form and be tolerated as a result of calculated responses. Therefore for Cat 3 structures supporting safety related plant, there is plastic yielding at certain sections and permanent deformation after the event. The behaviour is considered unsatisfactory if the relative deflections between points of support are greater than can be tolerated by the plant and services.

TABLE 1   PERFORMANCE CRITERIA

Performance Criteria	Structural Behaviour
1A	R.C. Liquid Containment, unlined or with a lining of low ductility.
1B	RC Liquid containment Structure with a ductile lining.
2.	Structure supporting safety related plant or services sensitive to deformations and their recovery.
3.	Structures supporting, or enclosing, safety related plant or services which are allowed to yield and have limited permanent deformation after the event.
4.	Structures not supporting, or enclosing, safety related plant and services but not impacting on other safety related structures, plant and services.

LINING TO ANCHORAGE DETAIL

FIG 4

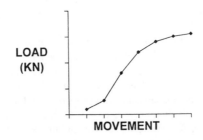

TYPICAL LOAD / DEFLECTION CURVE FOR ANCHORAGE

FIG 5

Lastly there was a requirement that structures not supporting safety related equipment must not impact onto other safety related structures, plant and services. It is assumed that there are no limitations on deformation, cracking and similar damage and the performance is only inadequate when the structure collapses.

Other components in the building are not safety related and may fail ~ eg Blockwork walls may collapse as long as they do not affect any structural or plant component required for safety.

The main loading combination for Cat 1 & 2 performance included normal operating temperature with the earthquake:

L = Dead + Live + Temp + Design Basis Earthquake

For Cat 3 & 4 performance, there were two changes:

(i) It is assumed that the plastic deformation of the steel reinforcement at hinges and across cracks relieves the induced temperature stresses. Also that the temperature strains are small in relation to those induced by the earthquake and does not affect the ability of the structure to absorb the energy.

(ii) The earthquake component is reduced by R - a response modification factor to account for energy absorption.

$$L = Dead + Live + \frac{Design\ Basis\ Earthquake}{Response\ Modification\ Factor}$$

The value of R depends on the type of construction, envisaged plastic behaviour and the detailing rules adopted and has been limited to 3 for Cat 3 structures on nuclear chemical plants.

Therefore the strategy is to identify the structural performance required and assign appropriate design criteria and load combinations - Table 1.

4.2 Stainless Steel Liners

A methodology based on ASME III Div 2 was required to ensure that stainless steel liners are not stressed beyond predetermined allowable limits during normal operating and extreme hazard conditions (6). The method of construction is to cast an anchorage grillage of 'T' sections into a structural screed in the base and into the walls of the cells. The base grillage is held in position by fixing it to adjustable stools which are bolted to the base concrete. In both directions the anchorage members are generally at 1.255m centres with specialist details around encast items and corners. the linings consist of 3mm thick type 304L stainless steel sheets which are cut to size, edges prepared for welding, then tacked to the grillages. The lining is completed by filling the gap with weld material which fuses the sheet and welds the sheet to the anchor Fig 4. If it is assumed that the lining is integral with the concrete surface, major stresses are set up in the liner due to:

(i) Thermal incompatibility between the concrete and stainless steel.

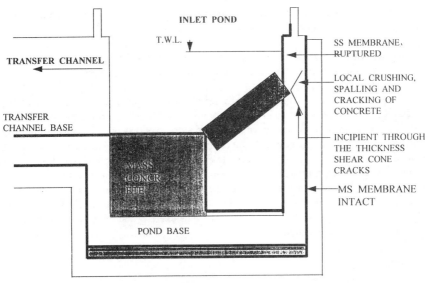

INLET POND

T.W.L.

TRANSFER CHANNEL

SS MEMBRANE, RUPTURED

LOCAL CRUSHING, SPALLING AND CRACKING OF CONCRETE

TRANSFER CHANNEL BASE

INCIPIENT THROUGH THE THICKNESS SHEAR CONE CRACKS

MASS CONCRETE

MS MEMBRANE INTACT

POND BASE

SIDE WALL IMPACT MECHANISM AND POSTULATED DAMAGE

FIG 6

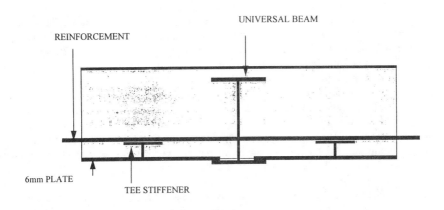

REINFORCEMENT

UNIVERSAL BEAM

6mm PLATE

TEE STIFFENER

PERMANENT SHUTTERING DETAIL

FIG 7

17

(ii) The bending of the wall and slabs including higher strains in outer liner member as it attempts to follow the movement of the concrete members.

To mitigate these stresses, it is necessary that a relaxation anchorage system is devised so that loads on the concrete structure are not passed directly to the lining system.

BNFL carried out a wide range of tests to determine the in-plane physical characteristics of anchorages with different types of connection from the 'T' into the concrete. The results varied some behaving very rigidly with little deflection whereas others withstood large plastic movement, Fig 5. The stiffness of the anchorage system was included as discrete springs and combined with the liner as rectangular plate element in a non-linear analysis. Results have shown that a low strength anchorage system is beneficial in ponds of a uniform nature with no cast in items. Where cast in items which may be thicker than the liner are present, high local stresses occur which may be relieved by detailing or the introduction of rigid attachments elsewhere. At edges, "soft" rounded corners are detailed so that there is no mechanical resistance to the in-plane loads.

4.3 Impact

On the Inlet Pond, small impact loads would easily breach the 3mm stainless steel liner. Therefore a second membrane was introduced between the concrete walls and foundations Fig 1. Calculations based on energy principles and empirical formulae gave confidence that a direct flask drop (150T) onto the bottom of the pond would not lead to any leakage. There was more uncertainty as to the effect of a direct dropped load on top of the pond, or an oblique impact on the side of the walls from a flask toppling within the pond. Fig 6. Therefore a scale factor of 1/10 was chosen to model the reinforcement, outer mild steel membrane and the concrete{7}. For the larger drop load, two models of the pond side wall were used to simulate the flask falling from +12m elevation onto the edge at +2m and impacting onto the wall. In each model, two tests were completed - one at mid span where the structure was most flexible and one at quarter span where the structure was stiffest. No permanent deformations were measured on the wall but two very fine cracks were visible on the outer surfaces, running to the top edges and being identified as flexural tensile cracks. The small average imprint depth of 1.3mm into the concrete wall (scaled to 13mm for the constructed wall) together with no permanent deformation led to the conclusion that the mild steel membrane would not suffer any significant damage. In all cases, dropped loads in excess of those physically possible were applied to establish design margins.

In the Chemical Separation area, dropped loads onto the cell roofs may cause small fragments of concrete to drop from the underside of the slab onto the structure's steel liner below and break the containment. To prevent this situation occurring, a plate was provided for the roof construction Fig 7.

5. QUALITY ASSURANCE

There is no doubt that Quality Assurance programmes have been beneficial in providing a disciplined approach to all activities affecting the quality of the design process right through to the finished structures and the production of documentary evidence to demonstrate that the required quality had been achieved. Other contributory factors have been the requirements to:-

(i) independently assess the structural design

(ii) phased approval of the design work by the NII, the final details of plant design not being complete when the base slab was constructed.

On the structural side, this naturally led the Head Designers to subdivide the building into areas and components, foundations, concrete cells walls and floors, in cell steelwork, out cell areas and steelwork superstructures etc and allocate areas of responsibility to individual engineers.

The engineers submitted packages to the Assessor for both the Approval of Major Analysis (AOMA) and the Approval of Design Calculations (AODC). The Assessors responsibilities were to approve that the methodology used by the designers was adequate for its purpose and that the analytical results were of the expected magnitude. In addition, a limited 5% of the calculations and drawings were inspected in detail to confirm that they met the designers intent. This emphasis on design philosophy encouraged the designers to document their approach on how and what they intended doing in the analysis and design stages. Statements of intent were produced by the analysis to cover the dynamic and thermal analyses of building illustrating the modelling techniques that would be used. Similarly Design Method Statements provided details of how the analytical output would be transferred into the design of individual members. These formal documents required engineers to think ahead and foresee possible problems at the later design stages.

Other aspects that have improved quality are:-

(i) Peer Reviews at the beginning of projects in the concept stage where identification of potential problems by experienced staff can lead to economic solutions rather than costly changes at later dates.

(ii) Verification and Validation of Computer Programs. This will continue to be an important area as computer costs drop and there is an increased usage of sensitivity studies to show the robustness of a design and the application of non linear analyses. A major problem will be limited amount of tests available to confirm the application of these models - a particular difficulty for the nuclear industry is the validation of soil structure interaction programs where many uncertain variables are involved.

6. SUMMARY

Over the years, BNFL has developed a systematic approach to risk management for the containment of liquid and aerial releases for normal operating conditions. Any leakage should, as far as is reasonably practicable, be detectable, collectable and quantifiable and there is a policy of defence in depth with multiple barriers. For aerial releases, the ventilation systems provide a differential pressure circulating the air from the lower active areas to the higher one - in case of malfunction the concrete cells, blockwork walls and exterior building cladding provide secondary containment.

On all projects, HAZOP studies are carried out by all functional disciplines and operational staff to identify the potential faults and related hazards that should be designed for. The major hazard affecting both the structure and the plant is the Design Basis Earthquake with a probability of 10^{-4} per annum - the sole concern is that the plant is in a safe state after the event but not necessarily operational. This allowed different performance criteria to be developed to ensure:-

(i) that the barriers are still effective

(ii) that structures supporting safety related plant have limited plastic deformation which will not affect the ability of the plant to perform its safety function.

In practice, there was a tendency to over categorise the building performance leading to conservative designs.

Another approach to dealing with uncertainty has been to support analysis work with physical testing. Experimental work was completed to establish the load/deflection of liner connections and non linear analysis carried out to confirm the adequacy of the stainless liners. Where there was uncertainty over the application of impact formulae, tests were carried to assess that cracking of the internal wall would not affect the mild steel membrane at the back.

The benefit of Quality Assurance has been that engineers have been made to document their approach and anticipate potential problems at an earlier stage rather than pressing ahead with the detailed studies. It is generally far less costly to include a design feature to restrict risk if it is included at an earlier stage of the process.

In the past, there has been a tendency to introduce additional safety features to produce conservative designs - it being more expedient to implement the change rather than justify whether it is required in accordance with ALARP principles. This can be attributed to the fact that the figures on the reliability of structures in earthquakes and the effect on radiological releases are very limited and specialised and therefore ALARP cases have to be demonstrated with wide margins to be successful and that a clear case has to be made. Economic pressures are now forcing us to look more closely at the cost of these safety features. It is felt that this situation of determining whether you should mitigate the risk by design features or demonstrate that it is not required by ALARP will be a problem facing other industries as they become more risk conscious.

7.   REFERENCES

1.   The Tolerability of Risk from Nuclear Power
     Stations - Health and Safety Executive   1988

2.   Safety Assessment Principles for Nuclear
     Plants - Health and Safety Executive   1992

3.   Safety Assessment Principles for Nuclear
     Chemical Plant - Health and Safety Executive   Oct 1983

4.   Safety Assessment Principles for Nuclear
     Power Reactors - Health and Safety Executive   April 1979

5.   Thorp Receipt and Storage Design
     and Construction - G W Jordan, A P Mann   Jan 1990
     The Structural Engineer
     Vol 68/No1

6.   Stainless Steel Containment Linings
     for Nuclear Processing Facilities,   1991
     W Jordan, L Denholm 'Civil Engineering
     in the Nuclear Industry' - Thomas Telford

7.   Design and Construction of the Inlet Pond
     Thorp Receipt and Storage Facility   1992
     Sellafield - G W Jordan, K R Clinton
     "Structural Design for Hazardous Loads"
     Institute of Structural Engineers

8.   ACKNOWLEDGEMENTS

The Author thanks A Campbell and B Howarth for their assistance in the preparation
of this paper and is grateful for the support of the Head of Department, Mr R T Day.

Risk Analysis For the Channel Tunnel

Douglas Parkes, Ove Arup and Partners, London
Charles Milloy, Ove Arup and Partners, London

INTRODUCTION

The Channel Tunnel was a very special project in many respects. The sheer size of the project coupled with the fact that it involved tunnelling an unprecedented undersea distance from the working shafts, gave cause for concern that all available means should be sought to limit the risks inherent in the undertaking. A series of safety planning measures were undertaken from the earliest days of the project and continued through to the detailed planning of individual operations during its execution. Today, no-one regards a risk analysis as unusual, but the majority of analyses are simple assessments of a qualitative nature. Few attempts are made to estimate risks probabilities in numerical terms. For the Channel Tunnel, detailed risk analyses were commissioned to calculate, in numerical probabilistic terms, the expected risk to life and limb of the construction personnel. The objective was to establish, to the satisfaction of the Health and Safety Executive, that these risks were not markedly greater than those which might be expected of a similar project on land. The special nature of the project justified the additional time and expense involved. The work which we describe was confined to the UK side served from the shaft and drifts at Shakespeare Cliff.

EARLY STAGES

Our firm became involved in some of the earliest preplanning work at the outset, and when TML were just beginning to set up the huge organisation necessary to execute the work.

At that time, the design of the marine service tunnel boring machine (TBM) was under consideration and ground and ground water conditions were foremost in the minds of the TML engineers. Figure 1 shows the cross section of the marine tunnels largely constructed in chalk marl. The chalk marl was expected to be reasonably dry and open-faced machines were considered to offer the best opportunities to achieve the high rates of progress needed to meet the target opening date; there remained the risk of encountering an uncharted borehole or some naturally occurring phenomenon that would connect the tunnel face to the sea and allow a catastrophic inrush of water. A probability analysis found the risk to be scarcely credible, however, the consequences were deemed to be so unacceptable that instructions were given to install special provisions on the open-face TBMs for the marine drives to assist in dealing with any inundation. Detailed emergency planning was also undertaken.

The planning and structural analysis of the machine components under emergency conditions resulted in detailed modification to the machine design.

These requirements aside, no specific provisions had been made in the TBM design (Figure 2) to allow for unusual risks, the design had simply to provide for a very high standard, capable of going the full distance with a minimum of downtime and to a good standard of safety for the operatives. Once the service tunnel TBM and its 200m backup train had been erected at the manufacturer's premises, we were asked to carry out a safety audit to identify risks in its

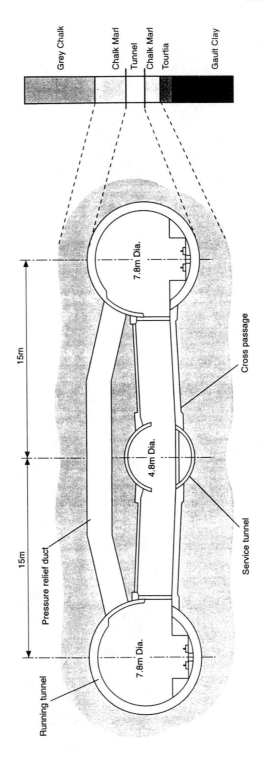

Figure 1   Typical Section Through Tunnel

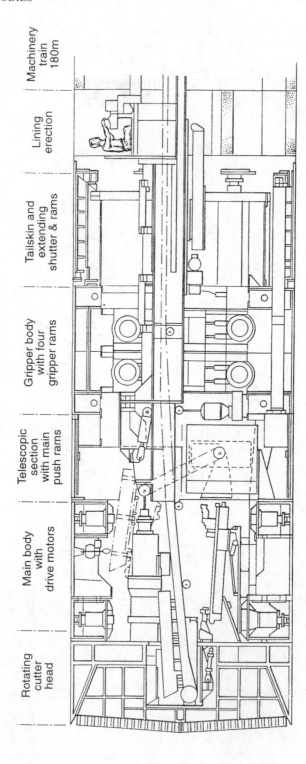

Figure 2   Tunnel Boring Machine for UK Marine Service Tunnel

operation and suggest improvements. Again, significant detailed changes were made to improve safety. One factor which remained however, despite measures to limit the possibility of ignition, was the risk of fire arising out of the use of mineral oil as the working hydraulic medium. This had been a cause for concern at the H&SE for some time, but TML and their machine manufacturer, Howden, considered that it was impracticable to change to a non-flam fluid. Not only would the wholesale replacement of components and seals have been necessary, causing high cost and unacceptable delay, but the lubricity, power transmission capacity and stability at high temperatures of the synthetic or emulsion-based oils then available made their use on such long drives impracticable.

Despite assurances, backed by the safety improvements, already achieved and a qualitative risk analysis carried out by TML staff, the H&SE remained unconvinced; a way had therefore to be found to quantify the risks involved in the project in order to compare them with what could be considered normal, if not acceptable, for tunnelling at that time. It was at this stage that it was decided that a quantitative risk analysis was required to determine the level of risk of injury or death during tunnel construction. The scope was widened to include all classifications of risk. A brief was then prepared and enquiries made, subsequent to which, our firm made the successful bid to carry out a full probabilistic risk analysis of the construction work. Initially this was confined to operation of the marine TBM, its backup train and the supporting tunnel logistics system, together with the following supplementary tunnelling work for openings, cross - passages, etc. A subsequent brief covered construction of the UK marine crossover cavern.

We believe this was the first time such an analysis had been carried out in tunnelling, certainly in the United Kingdom. The essential components of the Ove Arup and Partners team were the experience of systems reliability and rigorous probabilistic risk analysis gained in the British nuclear industry, and Bush and Rennie's intimate knowledge of practical tunnelling operations. This paper sets out to describe the service tunnel construction risk analysis, together with the subsequent risk analysis of the crossover cavern construction.

THE MARINE SERVICE TUNNEL

The tunnel system and TBM

The study covered the marine service tunnel and the cross passages construction and the completed sections of the marine service tunnel. The two running tunnels shown on Figure 1 are 7.6m diameter and the central marine service tunnel is 4.8m dia. The service tunnel was constructed ahead of the running tunnels and the cross passages built by hand in a follow up campaign.

RISK IDENTIFICATION AND CLASSIFICATION

A small team was set up in the TML office at Ashford under the general direction of the TML safety manager. Our team was able to benefit from an earlier TML safety audit and the initial few days were spent learning how the TBM operated and becoming familiar with the operational and safety planning. The aim was to create a logic-based model of tunnelling activities and possible mishaps which could result in serious injury.

The cooperation of TML staff was sought and readily provided; drawings, reports and procedures were studied. The construction planning was incomplete at that stage so a number of assumptions had to be made. Interviews were conducted with independent experts, researchers, public bodies and manufacturers representatives in the fields of systems and component reliability, fire, cables and hydraulics. A subcontract was let to Edinburgh University Fire Department to carry out desk research into the ignition characteristics of mineral oil. Close contact was maintained with H&SE throughout.

Some systems and component reliability information was obtained from our own data bank and from national and international reliability databases. There was, and still is, very little official accident data relevant to TBM tunnelling and reliability data was not available for some equipment. Engineering judgement had therefore to be applied where appropriate. Of necessity some of these judgements were subjective, but efforts were made to ensure that the assumptions erred on the side of pessimism. Whilst caution was required in regard to some of the lower ranking incidence rates, we were able to express confidence in the main conclusions and the recommendations made for improvement.

The first task was the systematic identification of all possible risks and their classification into generic areas. Although the original reason for the study was the perceived risk of fire, a conscious effort was made to treat risks of all types on an equal footing. Early qualitative work was reviewed and following discussions wit TML, staff five classifications of risk were selected:

o   Fire/explosion
o   Inundation/drowning
o   Mechanical shock
o   Electrical shock
o   Asphyxiation/poisoning

The detailed methodology applied to each hazard analysis is described in the separate sections that follow. Data on failure rates for times of plant was viewed in the context of the tunnel situation, and adjusted where appropriate. Frequencies of particular hazardous incidence occurring were derived for the five main hazards in the various work areas. Individual incidents in themselves may have a relatively low order of probability, but the summation gives an indication of the overall probability of a serious occurrence. In addition the largest contributions to the overall probability were identified to enable the greatest risks to be targeted.

FIRE/EXPLOSION

A serious fire was defined as an outbreak capable of causing loss of life or serious injury, which was not brought under control within five minutes. An explosion was considered to be an out-break of fire so sudden that fire fighting was not possible. The study did not distinguish between fire sizes, inasmuch as all serious fires were treated as presenting a hazard.

The TBM and machinery train were separated into zones, generally in accordance with the type of equipment present or the activity carried out there. A fire protection system was already planned for the TBM; single heat rise detectors were installed in zones sensitive to mineral oil fires, providing audible and visible warning for manual initiation of the sprinkler system, whilst double detectors were installed in electrical cabinets to cause, firstly, audible and visible warning and, finally, release of halon should both sensors trigger. Smoke detection systems were deemed to be reliable in all zones and independent human detection was considered according to occupation of each zone. The low expansion foam sprinkler system was manually operated and fitted with an overload protection system which prevented the (possibly panic) operation of too many systems at once causing the discharges to be ineffective. Hand-held foam and dry-powder extinguishers were also provided and hot work procedures required a fireman to be present the whole time.

The hazards listed in the initial assessment were subjected to a critical examination and supplemented following circulation and discussion with TML staff. The variety of hazard assessment techniques which could be used were then considered, and it was decided to use event trees supported by fault trees to provide branch probabilities.

The event tree developed to estimate serious fires is shown in Figure 3. This shows the development of the logic of combining the concurrence of flammable materials and ignition sources, followed by estimation of the probability of detection plus the probability that, once detected, it was successfully fought. This was followed through the 14 hazard zones on the TBM and backup train. Firstly the time fractions of each flammable material are estimated: the time fraction is the proportion of time that the flammable materials can be expected to be present. Some materials were permanently there, such as conveyor belting; others such as mineral oil aerosols are infrequent and their time fraction was derived from hose failure data and estimates of human response time. The time fractions of each material from the first branch of Figure 3 (T_m). The frequency of the material being ignited (λ_1) is then calculated by considering all the possible ignition sources and calculating the probability that each one will ignite the particular material in question. For example, a powerful spark ignites a mineral aerosol but sustained heating is required to ignite pvc conveyor belting. By combining flammable materials and ignition sources, the frequency of outbreaks of fire was calculated. An assessment was then made of the probability of the fire being detected by humans and the installed detector systems (P_D). If the initial fire was undetected it was pessimistically assumed that it will develop into a serious fire.

If it was detected, the probability of successful firefighting was estimated (P_F). λ_1, P_D and P_F are determined by solving small fault trees; the computations must take into account not only the whole range of ignition sources, detectors, etc and combine them in relation to each material in each zone, but must also consider the failure of fault detectors, poor maintenance and so on. The expected frequency of a serious fire can be calculated mathematically following the logic of the event tree.

A similar exercise was carried out for the construction of the cross-passages, and for the completed service tunnel and cross-passages for the time that they provided the supply route for the TBM and other works and were housing support electrical supply and pumping equipment. One of the basic assumptions made during the analysis was that there would be appropriate fire detection equipment in position within effective distance of possible conflagrations: the selection and siting of these items of equipment was the subject of a separate study at the time that the communications and emergency systems were being set up some months later.

27

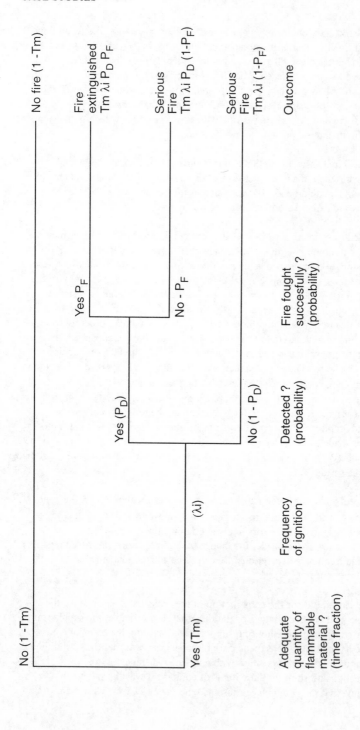

Figure 3   Fire - Event Tree

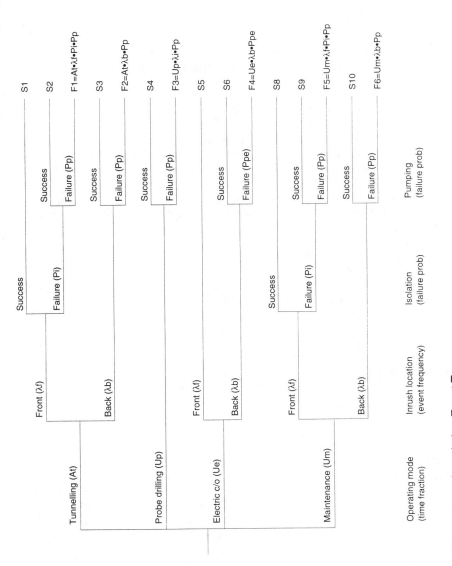

Figure 4   Inundation Event Tree

Several analysis runs were carried out, and the assumptions developed and adjusted after reviewing the results of each run. Expected frequencies of a serious fire were then re-checked for sensitivity to possible recommended improvements - the main contributors to the risk being set out in tabular form. The largest contributors to the fire risk were found to be conveyor belting, hydrogen and mineral oil. We concluded that every effort had been made to avoid unnecessary fire hazards in the TBM although the fire detection system could be improved. One very significant improvement was a ban on smoking, almost unheard of in tunnels at the time, which provided an almost fourfold improvement, and whicn was adopted by TML and now generally followed by the Industry. We were also able to recommend a series of improvements in planning, procedures and the provision of inexpensive but important supplementary equipment.

INUNDATION/DROWNING

This part of the analysis considered tunnel flooding due to sudden inrush of seawater in the unlined sections near the marine drive faces and at crosspassages. Three specific systems were to be provided to deal with an inrush of water: an hydraulically operated system which isolated the face area at the TBM, a set of segmental shutters to cover exposed ground at the rear of the TBM and an inundation pumping system to pump water from the TBM or any of the downhill drives to the surface. Various priority, override and isolation systems were to ensure their effectiveness.

The analysis followed a series of five stages, starting with identification of locations of possible inrush, TBM operating modes and preventative equipment, and construct a logic tree to represent event sequences (Figure 4). the frequencies of inrush events was then estimated, followed by the probabilities of failure of the isolation or pumping systems to operate effectively. Finally these values sere applied to the logic tree and the estimate of inundation frequency obtained. We found that inundation was very unlikely and, in the light of better information, that interception of an uncharted borehole was hardly credible. What did become apparent, however, was that the reliability of certain parts of the pumping system required significant improvement. Again, effective management, maintenance and testing procedures were demonstrated to be vital.

MECHANICAL SHOCK

This risk classification includes all the commonest causes of accidents in tunnelling, as in the rest of the construction industry. It was recognised at the outset of the study that the actions, movements and locations of individuals within the tunnelling system would be the major factor. A series of scenarios was established by considering the operation of the TBM, the method of construction of the cross-passages and the movement of trains in the tunnel. The nature and wide variety of this type of accident suggested that the most practicable approach was to develop each individually. Their frequency of occurrence could generally be estimated by a straightforward combination of base frequencies and probabilities, such that it was not necessary to adopt more complex fault or event tree methods.

The approach was to go meticulously through every move of the tunnelling crew members in the operation and maintenance of the machine, and in transferring between one activity and the next; to evaluate the times during which each was vulnerable to potentially injurious mishap and to combine this with incidence rates either drawn from recognised incidence and failure rate data or derived by engineering judgement from activity durations.

The analysis did indeed conclude that mechanical shock posed the most significant hazard to life and limb, and predicted a serious accident once in every two years at the peak of activity. Recommendations included the establishment of 'locking off' and permit-to-work/enter procedures in specific areas, in addition to those set up within the TBM itself.

ELECTRICAL SHOCK

This part of the study, perhaps more than the others, was very dependent on TBM and support service drawings, circuit diagrams, and machine and protective equipment specifications. A simple fault tree technique was adopted to take account of the coincident events which had to take place for someone to be electrocuted. Again, careful hazard identification was the first step, and the analysis was grouped under four separate headings: normal working, maintenance, accidents and feeder cable extension. The analysis showed that, barring the malfunction of isolation switches which are designed to be fail-safe, most of the failures would be due to human error, which was estimated subjectively.

We concluded that the risk of death by electric shock was quite low and that there was little that could be done to alter it by improvements in the equipment, which was of a very high standard indeed. We did emphasise, however, that the study assumed a very high degree of discipline in adhering to good practice and sound procedures, including permits-to-work, and the need for adequately and properly trained technicians for the work.

ASPHYXIATION/POISONING

The asphyxiation analysis was considered under three headings: inrush of deoxygenated air, ventilation failure and entering an unventilated space. The study was, of necessity, based to a large degree on subjective judgements, but was able to conclude that the risk of asphyxiation at the TBM was remote. However, the frequency of entry into unventilated spaces such as sumps and cross-passage reservoirs without adequate safety precautions was sufficiently high to warrant the recommendation of particular training of operatives in this respect.

ANALYSIS RESULTS
The results of the analysis are shown in Table 1 below.

HAZARD	RATE	ASSESSMENT
Fire/explosion	1 in 110 years	Low
Inundation/drowning	1 in 3500 years	Remote
Mechanical shock	1 in 11 years	High
Electrical shock	1 in 500 years	Low
Asphyxiation/poisoning	1 in 24 years	Medium
All hazards	1 in 7 years	High

Table 1: Marine Tunnelling Risks

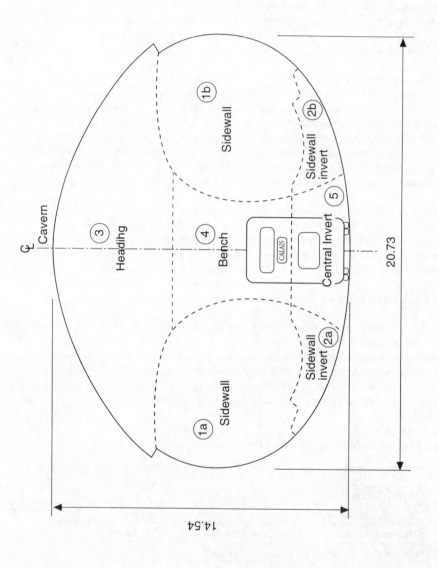

Figure 5   Cross Section of the UK Undersea Crossover

THE UK UNDERSEA CROSSOVER

Introduction

A crossover between the two running tunnels was required at approximately one third locations on both the UK and the French sides. The crossover permits the trains to change from the north running tunnel to the south and vice versa for operational and maintenance reasons. Because of their geometry size and location, it was not possible to construct the crossovers with the Tunnel Boring Machines and, after much thought, TML decided to use the New Austrian Tunnelling Method (NATM).

The UK crossover is almost 160m long, nearly 21m wide and 15m high. A drawing of its cross-section is shown on Figure 5 and the shape of double decker bus gives a good indication of the enormity of the challenge. The location of the cavern is vital to the alignment of the running tunnels and so its vertical and horizontal alignment and to be decided early on; and long before the ground could be investigated from the running tunnels themselves. Some information would be available from the service tunnel drive but extensive marine borehole investigation was unwise in case direct pathways to the sea were created.

At the chosen location, the cavern was expected to lie in the sound lower Chalk Marl and Gluaconitic Marl but the invert was in danger of entering the less reliable underlying mudstones. NATM was the only realistic construction method and TML asked us to carry out a risk assessment similar to that of the service tunnel TBM described above.

Our scope included the same five dangers as the service tunnel but it was clear that fires and explosions were less of a risk. An added concern was dust which had not been too bothersome in the service tunnel construction.

Figure 6 shows the intended construction sequence. In brief, two sidewall drifts were excavated and stabilised followed by a top heading. The inner faces of the two sidewalls were then incorporated into a bench followed by the excavation and construction of the invert. One construction cycle was taken to be the excavation of 1.5m of face; normally by roadheader followed by placement of steel supporting ribs, shotcreteing of the wall and subsequent rockbolting.

COLLAPSE/INUNDATION

After consideration, we decided to combine the treatment of collapse and inundation as one could to lead to the other. The lack of hard test data made it meaningless to use measured rock strengths at the base parameter from which to work. We had to invent another parameter which we could use to classify the variations in rock quality which we believed would be encountered and, if too weak, could demand modifications to the construction sequence.

The event tree on Figure 7 shows our approach. We adopted 'stand-up-time' as our basic parameter and decided, in conjunction with TML, that five rock qualities (excellent, good, fair, poor and bad) would be used. We judged that rockfalls would not happen for excellent and

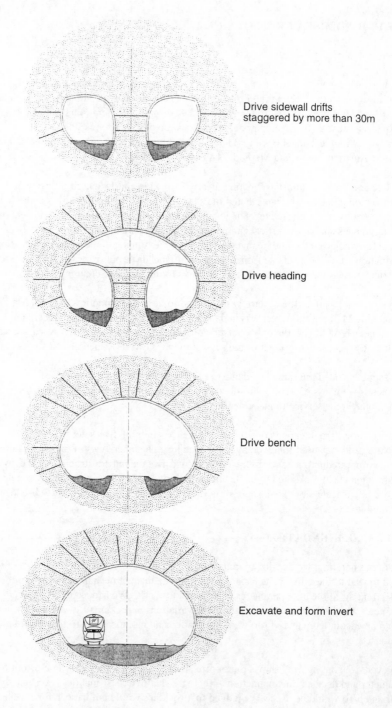

Drive sidewall drifts
staggered by more than 30m

Drive heading

Drive bench

Excavate and form invert

Figure 6   Crossover Construction Sequence

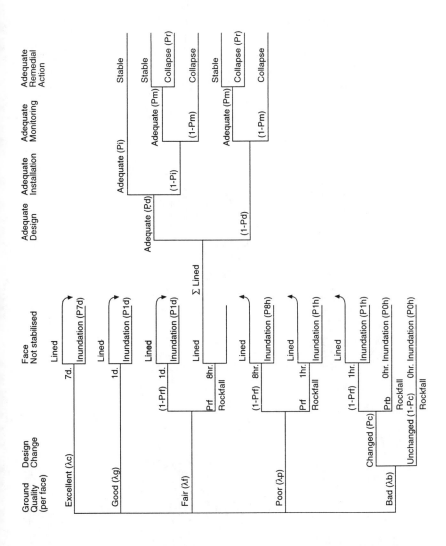

Figure 7   Inundation / Collapse Event Tree

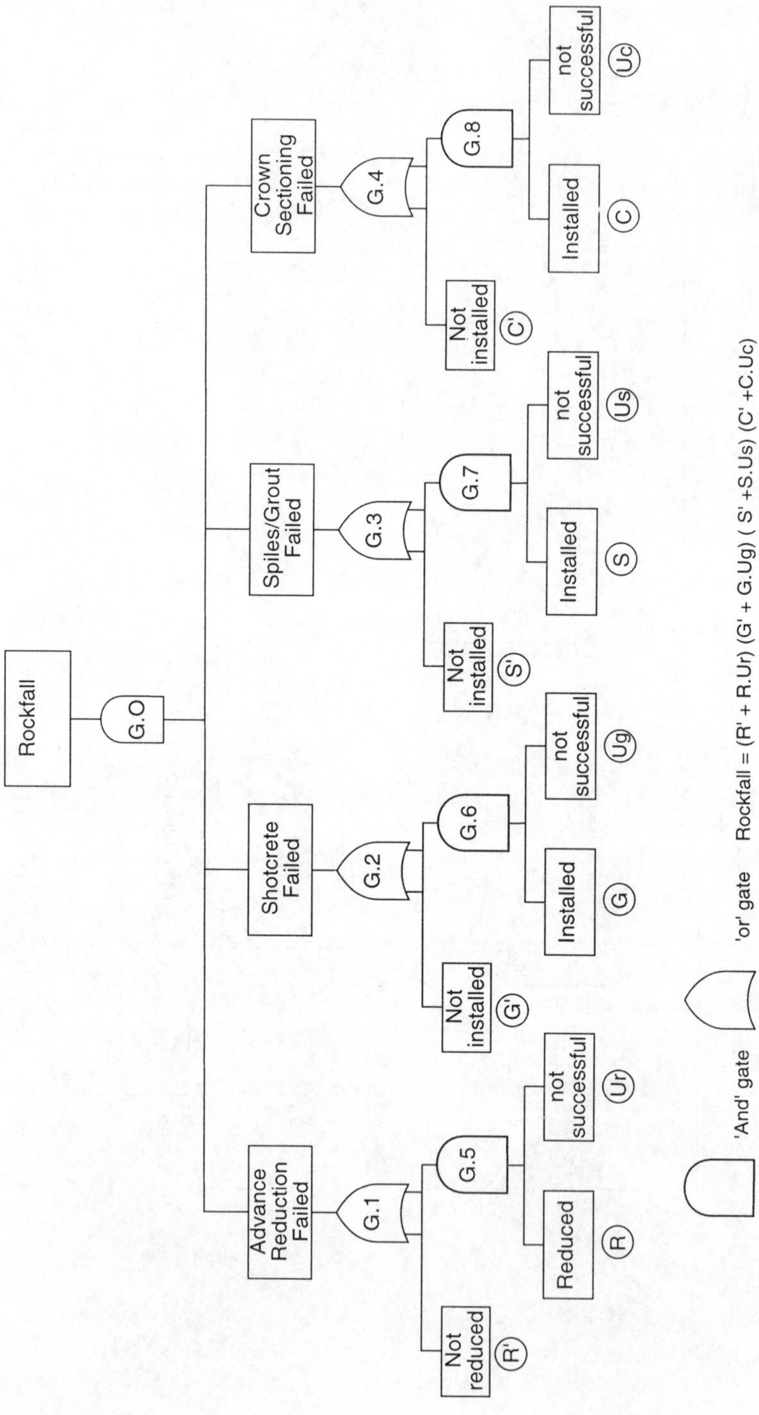

Rockfall = (R' + R.Ur) (G' + G.Ug) (S' +S.Us) (C' +C.Uc)

Figure 8 Rockfall Fault Tree

good ground which could remain for 7 and 1 day respectively before they would become unstable.

We considered that fair ground, where there had been no rockfall would stand up for 24 hours without treatment but that fair ground would only stand up for 8 hours if there had been a rockfall. Similarly poor ground would stand for 8 hours if there had bee no rockfall during a construction cycle but for only 1 hour if there had. On encountering bad ground, TML had indicated that they would modify the normal construction method and introduce one or more of the following variations:

- Reduce the advance length
- Shotcrete the face
- Use spiles and/or grout the rock
- Section the crown

The probabilities of failing to stabilise a face was modelled with the fault tree shown on Figure 8. Figure 7 shows the progression the analysis. Failure to install the temporary lining within the stand-up-time was deemed, rather conservatively, to lead to an unstabilised face which would create a crown hole, eventually leading back to the sea and possible inundation of the tunnels.

Deciding on the proportions for our stand-up-time proxy for each face was an act of faith. Following lengthy discussion among all involved and supported by the rock quality observed from the service tunnel, the categories were taken to be normally distributed.

The 7 month programme was broken down into half month snapshots and the planned progress at each half month was modelled. Fault trees were devised for each snapshot giving the combinations of failures which could lead to the face stabilisation being impossible. For example, the probabilities of there being no concrete, no power, no materials transport etc were estimated and used to calculate the frequency with which inundation might occur.

The statistical number of faces where inundation had been avoided were calculated and taken through to the next part of the risk analysis shown on the right hand side of Figure 7. In other words, having successfully lined the advance, the temporary lining could prove to be inadequate and need to be strengthened. At this stage, the design, workmanship, monitoring and management came under close scrutiny. By extensive interrogation of the planning, we felt able to allocate low probabilities that the design, temporary lining installations, lining movement monitoring and remedial actions would be unsuccessful.

ANALYSIS RESULTS

Mechanical shock, asphyxiation, fire/explosion and electrical shock were considered in a similar manner to the marine service tunnel and the results of the entire analysis are shown in Table 2 over the page.

The estimates show that Mechanical Shock (being hit by plant and materials) predominates; as would be expected. The risks of inundation and collapse are low and the identification and inclusion of additional, but inexpensive, back-up measures further reduced the risks.

HAZARD	RATE	ASSESSMENT
Inundation	1 in 370 crossovers	Low
Collapse	1 in 770 crossovers	Low
Mechanical Shock	1 in 7 crossovers	High
Asphyxiation	1 in 1600 crossovers	Remote
Fire/explosion	1 in 290 crossovers	Low
Electrical Shock	1 in 1400 crossovers	Remote

Table 2: UK Crossover Risks

CONCLUSIONS

All risks were estimated numerically and the initial concern over fire risk proved to be less of a problem. Thankfully, the risk of flooding was also shown to be small and, as anticipated, mechanical shock dominated. A number of safety improvements were identified and shown by reanalysis to be cost effective.

The risk analyses were carried out at an early stage in the planning. This had the great advantage that there was time for TML to take many of our recommendations on board and to modify, or supplement, equipment before tunnelling commenced. The chief disadvantage was that, occasionally, the planning was not fully developed.

We were, however, encouraged when we carried out the crossover cavern risk analysis where we found very careful and detailed planning had taken place.

Perhaps coincidentally, the safety record of the works was broadly in line with our predictions.

Risk-based Decision-Making in Bridge Maintenance

N C Knowles, W S Atkins Consultants Limited

The paper focuses on the use of formal decision-making methodologies to balance the competing interests of safety, direct cost, environmental and socio-political factors encountered in managing bridges. Application of the methodologies to the various maintenance options for a major motorway bridge structure is discussed.

It is estimated that there are some 155,000 bridges in public ownership in the UK. They are all subject to periodic inspection and re-assessment (to ensure continued fitness for purpose) where appropriate. For highway bridges the assessment programme is given added impetus with the introduction of the European 40 tonne vehicle.

Current structural assessment procedures provide little guidance about what to do if a bridge fails an assessment. The implications of 'failure' is that some sort of remedial action is needed, but the significance of failing an assessment may not be immediately obvious. Bridges fail assessments for a variety of reasons, but it is fairly unusual for signs of distress to be apparent and failure of an assessment does not necessarily imply that structural failure is imminent. The general feeling among bridge engineers is that assessments provide unduly conservative answers because the number of actual collapses of structures identified as approaching collapse is very low. A key question is thus how conservative is the assessment? How can this conservatism (ie. the likelihood of the bridge failing to meet its functional purpose) be quantified? Furthermore how should we account for the various consequences of such a failure? These two aspects (ie. the likelihood of failure and the consequences of it) are the key elements of risk - based methodology for prioritising bridge maintenance programmes.

Such a methodology not only has to recognise the inherent uncertainties involved in evaluating the risk to an individual bridge, but also that a number of different engineers are likely to participate in a programme of risk assessments. It is therefore important that the methodology is based, as far as possible, on objective (of subjective) measures of the contributory factors.

A complication is that the situation is not always 'steady-state'. For example bridges undergo continuous deterioration with time due to a range of deterioration mechanisms. Deterioration in bridges can be controlled, or at least minimised, by implementing carefully planned maintenance and repair schemes over the life of a bridge. Each such scheme will have a different risk 'profile'.

Depending on the condition of a bridge and the deterioration mechanism, a number of maintenance and repair options are available. These can be used in many different combinations over the life of a bridge to achieve an optimal maintenance plan. The safety of the bridge, disruption of traffic (which may be caused during extensive repair works), appearance of the bridge and public opinion are some of the important factors which need to be considered in choosing between alternative maintenance schemes.

Of equal importance is the problem of re-qualification of an old bridge (or a damaged bridge) which does not conform to the present day codes and standards. Available options in this case are: "use-as-is", repair, strengthen, reduce load rating, abandon or replace. Each of these options have significant implications in terms of cost, safety etc.

A further issue is the variety of ways in which information needed for decision making is expressed. In some instances 'hard' quantitative data may be available (eg. compressive strengths of concrete). In other instances the information may be qualitative (for example the corrosion is "severe"). Between the two extremes are a variety of methods which attempt to account for natural variability, incompleteness, ambiguity and inconsistency.

Against this background the need for rational decision-making is apparent. In general, the objectives of such decision making is to:

- assure the safety of bridge structures;

- preserve the road network capacity of minimising disruption to traffic;

- minimise the maintenance and associated (eg. indirect) costs in the long-term;

- optimise the spending of allocated funds (ie. prioritisation);

- secure the invested capital;

- maintain the appearance of structures, etc

A rational decision methodology should be able to satisfy all of the above objectives and be flexible enough to allow the decision-maker to assign different weighting to them depending on the individual situation. At the same time the overall decision-making process should be able to account for the wide diversity in the factors which influence bridge performance.

SESSION 1 : The Discussion

P A Merriman   Design Developments

D Parkes   Risk Analysis for the Channel Tunnel

N Knowles   Risk-based Decision Making in Bridge Maintenance

E Hambly I wish to present a challenge to the audience. I refer to a conference, in December, on Societal Risks at which a paper was presented by Keith Cassidy, the Head of Major Hazards Assessment Unit, HSE. The paper was on Assessment Regulation and the Public which began with the following sentence : 'Risk assessment, including quality risk assessment is perceived to fail to meet the needs of risk regulators, risk creators, risk analysts, risk commentators, risk communicators and the public, despite a very substantial effort on appropriate methodology and their application and use'. In other words we have some marvellous theories but in practice the problems are very different. I would therefore like to encourage contributions to discussion of what we can achieve effectively.

Mr Milloy, Ove Arup and partners.
I wish to add something to the debate about qualified and quantified risk assessment. The first point I would like to make is that any quantified assessment has always been a qualified assessment before it started. Nobody really pitches into a quantified assessment where you actually get the numbers out 10^{-3}, 10^{-4} , without having identified all of the hazards. You have to go from one to the other, it is a natural process. I think that sometimes you feel happier stopping at a qualified assessment and you spend a lot less of the client's money. However, if you do a quantified assessment you are actually sticking your head further into the lion's mouth. Sometimes it is necessary.

If you do a quantified assessment you are more or less obliged to be consistent because you have to think about every single number you put in. It forces you to make judgements, to be comparative, to say what you said yesterday and to look at what you said today and what you'll say tomorrow. Consequently, it does provide consistency.

To a very large extent it also requires you to make engineering judgement. Following Codes of Practice is something that everyone does initially, further on into their careers they are required, more and more, to make judgements when there is less and less help either from a textbook or from a Code of Practice. We are being quite brave by doing quantified risk assessment in order to make these judgements. But these judgements should be made only by people who are qualified to make them, because you have to justify every number you write down, you have to have it in a report, you have to say I have decided it is half because of the following reason.

You may even have to admit that it may be wrong and go on to explain why you don't think that is particularly important if you are. Obviously, sensitivity comes into it but you are forced to make a judgment and you are forced to recordand justify a judgement. Mostly, when things go wrong, it is not because someone made the wrong judgement it is because the judgement was not recorded in the first place, which takes me back to the importance of keeping formal records, something to go back to.

I would just like to concur with some remarks made earlier, about the infancy of this science. I think we all accept that it is in its infancy, it is like structural engineering was 150 years ago - not nearly as sophisticated and developed as it is today. But we have moved in that time and I don't think it will take us 150 years to get to the same level of competency that we now have in structural engineering.

Two points that I would like to finish with, because this conference is co-sponsored by Health and Safety Executive we must remember that economic risk is sometimes as important and sometimes totally important when there is no human life risk. The techniques we are talking about today can be equally used for economic assessments as they can for health assessments for safety of human life.

To finish with, I would like to comply with your earlier request for an example, Mr.Chairman.

At the moment we are doing work for a major utility in the UK; it is a control system for the whole of its national network. There are people within the organisation who are determined to have yet another Uninterruptible Power Supply [UPS] in the system. They have two already and this is the support for the computers. The analysis has shown that to buy another UPS would be a complete waste of money. So, I think we can advise them that they already have a very robust system, which does not need anymore UPSs. Therefore, the money would be better spent on upgrading other aspects of their system, which are less robust.

Mr.B.Neale, HSE.
I thought you might like to know what the law is saying to you about risk assessment, what it requires. What I will do in the time available is to metion one or two pieces of legislation and where they fit in. There are proceedings later that will enlarge upon this. The Health and Safety at Work Act, which to many still seems like a new act, is, in fact, twenty years old. I wonder how many of us have read it recently. It is not my intention to read the whole act but I would draw your attention to the phrase *reasonably practicable* and also the terms *safe, without risks to health* and *absence of risk*.

E Hambly, replying to Mr Neale
One cannot have absence of risk.

Mr Neale,
I agree. But The Act was drafted three decades ago and I was simply saying what is currently in the Act, this is where this debate goes forward and we try and manage that.
continuing.....
I would like to mention one other set of Regulations that some people may be aware of, The CDM regulations. They are out as many of you will be aware of and some information is included with the conference papers. Regulation 13 deals with the designers duties. Many of you will be designers, so please note the phrase 'to avoid foreseeable risks'. Regulation 13.2 introduces the phrase ' to combat at source risks' and Regulation 15.3 'safety plans' requires details of risks to the health and safety of persons to be taken into account and put in the

safety plan. So, here we are in the construction sector having legislation on risk that comes into effect at the end of March.

To put this in context we have the Health and Safety at Work Regulations, 1992, plus an Approved Code of Practice [ACOP]. This document draws attention to the need for risk assessments to be taken into acount, to identify necessary measures and deal with it. This is not just for construction, this falls under the Health and Safety at Work Act and applies to all work activities. To put that into context you mustn't just make the risk assessment, you must review it and amend it as the design of the job proceeds.

The document Management of Health and Safety at Work Act, including the ACOP, gives practical guidance on the principles that must be applied and how the various requirements for risk assessments under various regulations can be combined together. You don't necessarily have to redo assessments under one regulation when you have already done them under another, they can be combined together. In conclusion I would reiterate that there is a requirement under the Health and Safety at Work Act for assessment of risks; the main guidance that we have published is under the Management of Health and Safety at Work Act 1992 plus the ACOP.

A.Ellis, HSE.
I note the Chairman's remark but would emphasise the importance of the phrase 'as far as is reasonably practical'.

A. Leadbeater, Deputy County Engineer, Oxfordshire County Council.
I wish to refer to Mr.Knowles presentation. I have been involved with bridges for most of my working career. There are roughly 160 000 bridges in the country of which 135 000 are maintained by local authorities. 10 000 by the Department of Transport and Railtrack have approximately 15 000. I want to correct the impression made that bridge inspections are fuzzy, they are not, they are the first line of defence. If they are fuzzy and don't give decent information, then the bridge inspector hasn't been trained properly. I wouldn't accept that statement. Only three bridges have collapsed in service due to design failure since I started in bridges in 1958, including two footbridges in Hampshire. Many bridges have collapsed due to scour and due to impact on piers, the M50 motorway, for example, where several lives were lost.

Bridge bashing has caused a lot of deaths. We had one in our county only three months ago, at a site where warning signs were up. The lorry hit the bridge and fell over onto a car killing the occupant. If there had been four occupants in the car there would have been four people killed.

Landslip and mining subsidence also causes collapse of bridges. I have to point out again at this point that other countries don't do work on maintenance of structures and that accounts for the increased number of bridges that collapse on the continent and in America (the Chairman added 'and recently in Korea').

I think the problem of local authority bridge engineers and Department bridge engineers is one of credibility. We have got increased loading of bridges coming along. Many old bridges, probably 60 000 of those 160 000 bridges I referred to earlier, are at least 70 years old. Each time the loading increases the inbuilt factor of safety reduces but, unfortunately, nobody really knows what the inbuilt factor of safety is. We have a National Assessment Code, it is highly numeric, it is very suitable for putting on a computer and gives answers. But it doesn't allow for engineering judgement. My basic point is that if you adopt a numeric system without exercising engineering judgement there are going to be extreme difficulties because bridges that don't need strengthening and don't need maintenance will, in fact either be restricted or repaired, which is undesirable.

E. Chaplin, Tarmac Construction.
A very general question : as an industry we accept that absolute safety is unattainable, an elusive goal but we also accept that we have to manage and identify all risks. At some point the resources we devote to this exercise in reaching this elusive goal must reach a stage at which society will say enough is enough. Can I ask Mr.Ellis are we approaching that stage now ? and if not does this reaching or this attainment of this elusive goal go on ad-infinitum ?

A.Ellis, HSE.
I suppose if you look back over the history of safety you see a gradual tightening of standards. But I hope you see a tightening where, in a sense, there is a proven need for that tightening. The particular advantage of risk assessment, while it may have some new features in the particular industries we are discussing today - for instance in the chemical industry, is that it can target where the money is best spent. Now, we have numerous examples where there was an overall need to improve off site safety, in the aftermath of, say Bhopal, and accidents like that. When you carry out your risk assessment you can see exactly the elements onsite that cause a particular level of safety offsite. You can start to see where you obtain most return for your money. There are enormous opportunities to save money in doing that.

There was enormous concern in the chemical industry, when these techniques arose in the first place, because they saw it as creating a huge capacity for retrofitting safety which would be enormously expensive. I think what many in the industry now see is that there are many advantages for those doing these projects, the industrialists, the builders and the designers as indeed there are for the regulators in trying to get most return for the money.

E Hambly
I think the chemical industry is one where they are able to remove the men from the manufacturing process. You gave earlier a statistic of tolerable risk at work of 1 in 1000 per year. In the construction industry we have a safety record that is actually ten times better than that. Hence the question arises as to why we need these regulations if we are already performing reasonably well.

A.Ellis
Clearly I don't wish to give an answer that only applies to a particualr area of regulation. Speaking generally where there is an anxiety at a particular level of safety in a particular industry where there is political anxiety or public anxiety then there is the drive for improved standards.

E Hambly
Let me push a little further. I have a feeling that the level of accidents on construction sites nationally approximates with the average riskiness of daily life and this is where I am coming back to the randomness of human nature and so on. I question whether the regulations will make construction safer or whether the use of mechanical rather than manpower would be equally effective.

A.Ellis
It is really effective planning again.

E Hambly
We've had fifteen years of no improvement in statisitics and great improvement in planning.

A.Ellis
One of the advantages that is coming forward now is trying to get much more structured safety thinking into large engineering projects.

E Hambly
That I agree with, we can all develop techniques for anticipating hazards.

D.Mclean, Capital Housing, Edinburgh.
A question for Mr.Merriman : referring to snow loading you said quickly, in passing, that you just went up and removed it. Given the height and exposure of these buildings could you explain how this is done ? Has any thought been given to modifying the roof shape ? or combining it with a heat recovery system ? an ideal way to harness waste heat.

P.Merriman, BNF plc.
There will be an early warning for extreme snow loads from the meteorological centres. It is assumed that the site staff will have sufficient notice of a build up of snow loads, to allow them to clear the roofs. If the purlins should fail, the possibility of impact damage on the thick concrete cells and mechanical equipment below is considered in the safety case, and there may be no radiological consequences. Therefore, there may be no safety requirements to design the purlins for the extreme loads. No thought has been given to modifying the shape of the roof, as the present design is adequate for the purpose.

B.Lee, University of Portsmouth.
A point of correction. with regard to the snow loading on the roof, the dominant criterion is not the height of the snow on the roof. It is the occurrence of a heavy rainfall after snow has fallen and you may get little warning of that.

E Hambly
Mr.Merriman, you talked about having a 10 000 year return period and you compared it with a 50 year return period. With a 50 year return period people use safety factors, what does this mean for the run of the mill problem. A structure could be designed for a 50 year return period with a safety factor of 2 and this might be adequate for the 10^4 case.

P.Merriman

In conventional design, for the 50 year return period, appropriate factors are included in the load combinations and material factors to cater for uncertainty. On nuclear chemical plants, designed for more extreme events, the load factor is taken as 1.0 for the DL+ LL+Eearthquake case, with design criteria varying according to the structural performance required. Buildings not designed specifically for seismic loads will carry loads equivalent to 0.05g to 0.10g zero period acceleration.

L.Howe, AEA Technology.

I would like to make a comment on what all the speakers have said this morning. When you do a risk assessment this doesn't give you the answer, it helps you to understand the problem. We heard this morning about multivalue attribute analysis - what that helps you to do is to is to understand the importance that you attach to things. It is no use doing a risk analysis if it is not part of a risk management programme, where you actually understand what effects your management actions take.

The other point that I wish to add is that the identified threats either happen or they don't. It is all very well having a deterministic approach of likelihood times impact but what you have really got to ask yourself is whether it is likely to happen, does it happen ? doesn't it happen ? and what happens ? rather than just multiplying the two input parameters together to give you a risk analysis.

E Hambly

I would like to address a question to Douglas Parkes. On the cross over cabin you had a problem of a blister developing on the roof I believe. Did your risk assessment help you to react to it?

D.Parkes, Ove Arup and partners.

What the risk assessment did was to identify that type of problem and then probe the details of the planning that was in place to deal with it, together with the reliability of the systems that were in place to support it, to and give it a reasonably clean bill of health. In fact what happened was more or less what was predicted. There were aspects of the way in which water pressure had been dealt with in the design and in the investigation : it was difficult to find out what it was likely to be and that was the thing physically which caught them out, if you like, temporarily. The emergency measures that were in place to deal with that, which was relieving the water pressure and then strengthening the support appropriately, coped with the situation. Hence, the risk analysis was, in fact, a supplement to the planning that was in position and it happened more or less how we all thought.

J.Mann, Railtrack.

Speaking personally, I am concerned about this desire to quantify everything. What Mr.Parkes said about scarcely credible risk intrigued me because the consequences were deemed to be unacceptable, so we are back to engineer's judgement.

I would like to illustrate it very briefly with a case history. When the Severn Tunnel was being driven, over a hundred years ago, the Engineer realised that, in view of the ground conditions that were being found and the unexpected ingress of water, it was going to be a good idea to alter the design. It was a very shallow Vand he decided to drop the apex of the V - I forget the exact figure, 15 - 20 feet below the bed of the river, because he thought there was a real risk of a collapse of the river bed. When they dropped the level a scarcely credible risk came into play because they tapped an underground river. We are still pumping that water out of the Severn Tunnel.

With that marvellous creature hindsight, if we'd known all that, I wonder what the level of the tunnel would have been today ? Clearly it would have been cheaper to construct the tunnel at the original level, we wouldn't have been faced with all the pumping and the risk of being that much closer to the river bed might have been acceptable.

E Hambly
There is really an excellent book in the Institution's library by the contractor, a man called Walker. In constructing the Severn Tunnel, because of the risk that has been described, they dropped a heading right to the middle under the central channel and excavated from the centre outwards. They thought that if they were going to lose the tunnel, they preferred to do so at the beginning. It is an interesting description of risk assessment being used in deciding a construction sequence.

D.Chamberlain, City University.
My feeling is that the construction industry is not that safe if one looks at the life-health of the workers. If one looks at the States we see that upper muscular skeletal problems later in life has a greater level of incidence in construction workers. If we think of steel bridge restoration now, we see people removing substances such as zinc chromates which are known agents for cancer. In the States, where I have spent some time looking at these issues, the life health is having to be covered by insurances. This is leading to high fees for work. I suspect we are still protected from that and in the long run things will cost a lot more when the true cost of health is known.

J.Menzies, Standing Committee on Structural Safety.
I wanted to refer to your earlier comment Mr.Chairman regarding the risks associated with the construction industry being approximately the same as those in everyday life and I would like to address a question to Mr.Ellis. My understanding, and I'm no authority in the field, is that in the manufacturing industries the risks have been reducing gradually over the years and continue to reduce. My understanding is that this is not the case for the construction industry and the statistics, which have already been mentioned, show that the risks have remained constant. Perhaps Mr Ellis could comment on that.

Mr Ellis
The construction industry is not my background and I suggest a more authorative answer might possibly be obtained from a member of the audience.

R.Evans, HSE.
I don't have the detailed statistics immediately to hand but I do have responsibility for the construction industry. As I recall, if you take the fatal accident incident rate going back to the 1960's and compare it with the fatal accident rate over the last few years the trend has been significantly down, more or less entirely over that period. The industry is now operating at a level of probably one half that it was operating under in the 1960's. To put that in context, it is still some three or four time more hazardous to work in the construction industry than it is in

other manufacturing industries. But the record has improved and I think that anyone who has worked in the industry for a long time will recognise that simply by walking down the high street and looking at the things that you can see, the control of risks has been greatly improved over that time span.

One of the arguments that we used in relation to the Construction Design and Mangement regulations and the need for those Regulations, in order to make a step-improvement in that record, was that we actually needed an overlay of management responsibility in order to control risks. I think it is very interesting that this conference is about the management of risk, it is not simply as one might be forgiven for believing from some of the detailed discussion about risk assessment. I would like to echo the comment of a previous questioner that risk assessment is a means to an end it is not an end in itself. It is the management of the risk process that we ought to be concerned with.

While the accident record over time has certianly improved quite considerably, there is no room for complacency. Comparison of HSE national figures with European figures shows that our record so far as one can compare like with like is roughy equal to France and Germany.

N.Stockton, ICI.
I would like to make a comment on the comparison between the construction industry and the manufacturing industry. I actually believe this stems from beliefs. The manufacturing industry is in fact a globally international competitive industry and there is a belief in the industry that to be world class competitor one has to have a world class safety performance. So there is a belief that a good safety performance goes hand in hand with a good company. I would question whether those beliefs are currently held in the construction industry.

E Hambly
I am sure they are held. And I am sure construction companies see it as a source of pride. Metal forming industries have a record very similar to construction because they are manual. The ones that have low statisitics have very much less activity.

Jill Wilday, HSE.
My comment goes back to when I was working in the chemical industry. Back in the 1980's the chemical industry was noting that its accident rate had been falling and had levelled off. The way it got it to continue to fall was to concentrate on safety management. This is, in effect, saying we accept you cannot infinitely reduce risk to zero but in terms of how we manage our company, we are going to set a target of zero accidents and get the whole culture of the company to accept that. That actually brought the accident rate down further. Even though, technically speaking, zero risk is an impossibility, aiming for it is still a good idea.

SESSION 2
Current developments of
risk assessment methodology

Process Re-engineering for Safety

Professor David Blockley, University of Bristol

Engineering is basically about making things - artefacts and systems of artefacts from large power stations to hand held computers. Good engineering requires quality which, expressed in its simplest form, is fitness for purpose. More formally quality is the conformance to predetermined requirements (ASCE 1988). Quality assurance is one means by which we try to ensure we reach this objective but unfortunately it often seems to breed bureaucracy. QA is not enough. We also need quality management which is based on incremental improvement and well supported processes. However recent management thinking is that this is not enough either and that it is often necessary dramatically to re-design or re-engineer company processes to establish or keep a niche in an increasingly competitive world of constant change. The re-engineered processes have to make the best use of scarce resources and to incorporate IT (Hammer and Champy 1993).

The quality requirements to be considered in the design, construction and operation of artefacts are many but primarily they can be classified as function, safety, reliability, economy and aesthetics. The provision of safety and reliability is therefore one part of quality management. The construction industry has a very poor safety record. Safety has therefore to be a central objective of construction business process re-engineering (BPR). Since the connection between lack of safety and real cost has now been directly demonstrated (HSE 1993) the BPR currently being undertaken by many of our companies provides a new business opportunity to incorporate safety as a direct business benefit.

Uncertainty

At the root of safety and reliability is risk and at the root of risk is uncertainty. Uncertainty can be classified as *FIR (Fuzziness, Incompleteness and Randomness)*. To deal with uncertainty we must build models of it. These can be the subjective 'mental models' we all carry with us or the more 'objective' models available through shared theory. Most developed risk models incorporate probability theory as a measure of randomness. However little has been written directly about just exactly what is meant by randomness. Here we will follow Karl Popper by defining the *randomness* in a piece of information as the lack of a specific pattern in that information. Patterns are detected by ingenious testing and so the more tests the information fails then the more confident we can be that it is random. Any one test that finds a pattern demonstrates non-randomness. In that sense the search for non-randomness is analogous to the search for truth (Blockley 1980). *Fuzziness* is imprecision of definition which was identified and mathematised by Zadeh (1975). This treatment of fuzziness has grown into a discipline of its own. For example fuzzy controllers are now used in a range of products. *Incompleteness* is that which we do not know and hence cannot be modelled. Since a model is by definition not the reality it is partial and incomplete. Thus although there are advanced theories to model randomness and fuzziness these theories are essentially incomplete. Unfortunately failures are often the unintended consequences of human action (Blockley 1980). It is imperative therefore that uncertainty is perceived as something to be managed not as something only to be predicted. Of course that is not to argue that predictive calculations are not useful, rather that they provide evidence in the management of uncertainty and hence in the management of safety risk and hazard.

Hazard

Turner (1978) argued that large scale accidents usually have multiple casual factors which accumulate over a considerable period of time called an *incubation period*. For example events may be unnoticed or misunderstood because of the wrong assumptions about their significance. Dangerous preconditions maybe unnoticed because of the difficulty of handling information in complex situations. There may be uncertainty about how to deal with formal violations of safety regulations. When things do start to go wrong the outcomes are typically worse because people tend to minimise danger as it emerges, or to believe that the failure will not happen. As a result, events accumulate to increase the predisposition to failure. The "size" of the trigger event (eg. a high wind, an earthquake or a simple human error) which releases the energy pent-up in the system, is not the only important cause of the accident, rather one of the main tasks is to identify the preconditions. These preconditions are the hazard and they represent the developing 'potential' for failures and accidents.

Definitions

One reason that the discipline of safety engineering is not yet 'mature' is that there is no agreed set of definitions. Another reason is that the relationship between technical and human and organisation factors is not yet worked out. The topic could be said to be 'adolescent' in the sense that those involved are gradually becoming aware of it's limitations.

A hazard is usually defined as a situation that has the potential of human injury, damage to property, damage to the environment or economic loss (Roy Soc 1992). More specifically EERI (1984) defines *seismic hazard* as "any phenomenon associated with an earthquake that may produce adverse effects on human activities". Note that these definitions are subtly different from the concept described in the previous section since there is no suggestion of process ie. that hazards incubate.

Risk is usually defined as the change of a defined hazard or the probability of a defined hazard and the magnitude of the consequences (Roy Soc 1992). More specifically the United Nations Office of the Co-ordinator of Disaster Relief (UNDRO) defined *earthquake risk* as "the expected losses to a given element at risk, over an specified future time period" (Coburn and Spence 1992). EERI (1984) defined seismic risk as "the probability of social or economical consequences of earthquakes will be equal to, or will exceed, specified values at a site, at several sites, or in an area, during a specified exposure time". Both definitions are partial and complementary. For example, a factor that is not considered in both of the definitions is the context in which the losses are expected.

Note that in these definitions of risk the hazard is the failure or trigger event. However this is a partial definition since hazard should be considered as the rather more general concept, described earlier, involving external factors as well as the characteristics of the structure itself. Hazard is a group of characteristics, external or internal to the system, that individually or together represent a developing current state of affairs which could result in an unacceptable future state of affairs. It is that future state of affairs that is the hazard or trigger event. Of course this implies that it is possible to project some future scenarios leading up to the trigger event which may cause damage. However it is not possible to predict **all possible** future scenarios. Since many failures are the unintended and unforeseen consequences of human actions (Blockley 1992) a risk prediction may not include the events that actually cause failure. Thus risk analysis is essentially incomplete.

As a result a risk has been defined as the combination of the chances of occurrence of some failure or disaster and its consequences in a given context (Blockley 1992). The fundamental problem with risk analysis is that the projected number of future scenarios is infinite and the calculus of probability theory assumes completeness. Note that there is no implication that risk prediction is not useful only that risk prediction is partial.

Safety is defined as freedom from unacceptable risks of personal harm (Roy Soc 1992). More generally it is freedom from danger where danger is hazard of personal harm.

EERI (1984) defines vulnerability as "the degree of loss to a given element at risk, or set of such elements, resulting from an earthquake of a given magnitude or intensity, which is usually expressed on a scale from 0 (no damage) to 1 (total loss)". This is a loss function. However the vulnerability of a structure should be a function of the form of the system and the way in which it is susceptible to damage by any arbitrary action (Wu, Blockley, Woodman 1993). The analysis of the susceptibility of failure is concerned with the identification of "weak links" in the form of the structure and the derivation of a particular future scenario (most likely, maximum or minimum failure scenario and so forth) in which the structure is damaged under any arbitrary action. Of course if attention is restricted to a particular type of action then the vulnerability must depend on the nature of that action. Thus for example, in earthquake engineering, seismic vulnerability analysis concerns the identification of particular scenarios in which the most damage results from any arbitrarily small earthquake.

Thus in summary it is important to see safety, risk and hazard in term of the process by which safety is ensured by directly managing hazard and thus indirectly managing risk. In order to manage hazard evidence from the past, present and future has to be collected. In this context risk analysis is the business of collecting evidence about certain foreseeable future scenarios.

Process

The current interest in business process re-engineering (BPR) is helpful to the business of hazard management. BPR invites us to re-examine the business by focusing on process rather than function. An essential element of BPR is the intimate involvement of IT.

Within IT applications currently there is much interest in the modelling of product information (eg. Bjork 1989) to enable common standards for communication between data bases. Likewise there is much interest in process modelling. The motivation of this is that appropriate support for business processes within a company will increase quality, enable business re-engineering and hence reduce the risk of failures and accidents.

The aim of process modelling is to provide an integrated computer based environment which will support managers in fulfilling their roles and will provide real business benefits. The intention is to help co-ordinate the activities of people and the ways in which information is transferred in and between companies. The feasibility of using Process Support (PS) systems to aid Quality Management (QM) in civil engineering design has recently been examined (Platt & Blockley 1993).

A process is simply a task, albeit a long and complicated one and separable into many activities, carried out using resources and resulting in deliverables. Process modelling is a way of representing on a computer certain kinds of activities in the actual world. These activities occur within an organisation in which there are people who have obligations to fulfil, tasks to carry out and tools to help them. The idea is to capture the organisation of the processes of meeting responsibilities and carrying out activities using a modelling language. Execution of the model prompts users to perform activities in accordance with their roles in the organisation and provides them with accurate and up to date information. The process model handles the sequencing of activities and is continually changing as people define and redefine activities in response to changes. For example a new project will spark off a new set of activities. A process model must be dynamic, its existence and evolution are dependent on interactions with the people whose responsibilities it models.

Management of Hazard

At any particular moment, the state of a project is characterised by a set of conditions or a state of affairs, the hazard. Once the preconditions for unwanted futures are identified, the three Rs of the hazard incubation process management are proposed as:-

1) *Remove the hazard*
2) *Reduce the hazard*
3) *Remedy the hazard*

To illustrate, imagine that the hazard is a banana skin on the floor in a corridor. A *remove* action would be to throw it in the bin. (Note that the risk analyst would attempt to calculate the probability that the next person to walk down the corridor would slip on the banana skin and injure himself - but that is unnecessary). Of course the remove alternative is now always available. For example if the banana skin is a seismically active region such as Tokyo or Mexico the hazard cannot simply be removed. The next alternative is to *reduce* the hazard by conceptually redesigning the situation. Thus we might erect a fence or put a warning notice in the corridor about the banana skin or we might strengthen buildings in a seismic region. The final option is a *remedy* action which involves tactical change. For example a defensive option would be to make the situation safe by throwing sand over the banana skin or by controlling the detailed seismic characteristics of buildings. Of course the remedy and reduce alternatives are actions that may be taken based on the results of a risk analysis. This analysis is therefore an aid in the direct management of hazard for the indirect management of risk.

Evaluation of Proneness to Failure

A general method of an assessment of hazard has been described by Sanchez-Silva, Taylor and Blockley (1994) and applied to seismic regions. The problem is to evaluate the "proneness to failure" of a particular project due to a future (seismic) event. One of the objectives is to identify the vulnerability of a project by searching for the "weak links". Since damage is anything that causes some loss of function the search for hazard is the search for potential and actual accumulating damage. The method of effectively a series of tests (such as audits) which a project must pass in order to be declared dependably safe. Dependability is a concept (Blockley 1980) based on the work of Popper on the corroboration of scientific theories. The development of corroborated scientific theories (leading to true theories) depends upon the ingenious testing of hypotheses. Similarly, the development of dependable projects (leading to safe projects) depends upon ingenious testing of all phases of the project. Thus dependability was suggested as a measure of the degree to which an engineering theory has been tested in practical decisions. The converse of dependability is vulnerability which accrues over time by accumulation of factors, which produce the preconditions for failure. Vulnerability is increased if the project does not pass critical tests either through the tests not being carried out, or failure to meet the criteria for passing the test (Comerford and Blockley 1993). There are three types of test, past, present and future. Evidence collected about the past and present is combined with projected future scenarios (risk analysis (Dester, Blockley 1995).

Safety Culture

One important factor in the assessment of hazard is safety culture. It is known that the construction industry has a poor safety record and that there is a common perception that this is because it is an inherently dangerous industry. Dester and Blockley (1995) have suggested that the industry would be better characterised as one with a poor safety culture and that attempts to improve the safety record will not be fully effective until the safety culture is improved.

In various guises, poor safety culture is now being recognised as a significant factor in the development of accidents and disaster. The CBI (1990) also linked a good safety culture with profitability. Since culture was defined as "the ideas and beliefs that all members of an organisation share about risk, accidents and ill health". Butler (1989) described the need for a fundamental change in corporate culture with regard to safety. Heiermann 91988) suggested that employers need actively to develop safety consciousness which he defined as "the preparedness and capability of recognising danger, estimating the likelihood of an accident happening, and its extent, and acting correspondingly". Steiner (1987) referred to safety climate as "intangible safety attitudes and perceptions" while describing a means for its assessment. Here, safety culture is defined as the set of beliefs, norms, attitudes, roles and social technical practices which are concerned with minimising the exposure of individuals, within and beyond an organisation, to conditions considered dangerous or injurious, (Pidgeon, Turner, Blockley and Toft 1991). Since safety is part of quality (Blockley 1992) these ideas are closely linked with quality culture and management and hence directly with profitability and success.

Practical Learning

The ingredients of a good safety culture are similar to those of a quality culture. The following acronym 'practical learning illustrates some of the important factors that are present in a company with a good safety culture.

P   *Point of view* - remember we all have one and should respect those of others

R   ensure *Responsibilities* and accountabilities are clearly defined

A   encourage positive *Attitudes*

C   have good *Communications* - both formal and informal

T   ensure the *Technology* is appropriate

I   have clear *intentions* or *objectives*

C   show a *Caring* approach to safety (especially needed in senior management)

A   keep all workers *Aware* of quality and safety issues

L   encourage a *Learning* approach with an open mind - see failure not as a cause for blame but as an opportunity to learn

E   give *Encouragement* - give praise at every **genuine** opportunity

A   keep Auditing by testing hazard - measure and check through performance measures

R   keep a firm grip on *Reality* - don't allow yourself to be deluded, keep your feet on the ground, face facts don't shy away from them

N   encourage *new ideas* - help people to be creative in `owning' and hence changing processes to clear objectives

I   make *Information* as clear and unambiguous as possible using IT wherever appropriate

N   have *No yes* men - truth is found from honest disagreement amongst friends

G   be *Genuine,* honest and open

Re-engineering the organisation

Hammer and Champey (1993) outlined a few simple rules for considering the re-engineering of an organisation. They are:-

- where possible combine several jobs into one

- allow workers to make decisions - empower them, flatten the company hierarchy

- speed up processes by looking for concurrency

- recognise that there are multiple versions of processes - set up appropriate criteria

- work is best performed where it makes most sense - don't let organisational boundaries slow up the process

- reduce checks and controls to the minimum but have clear performance measures

- minimise reconciliations use IT to help design systems that reconciliate

- have one single point of contact - a case manager for the process

- have hybrid centralised/decentralised operations - use IT for standard information systems and processes such as procurement

Hammer and Champey argue that in this new world of work the changes are that:-

- work units change - from function to process;

- jobs change - from simple tasks to multidimensional ones;

- people's roles change - from controlled to empowered;

- job preparation changes - from training to education;

- focus of performance measures changes - from activity to results;

- advancement criteria change - from performance to ability;

- values change - from protective to productive;

- managers change - from supervisors to coaches;

- organisational structures change - from hierarchical to flat;

- executives change - from scorekeepers to leaders.

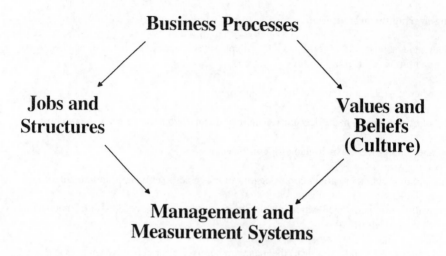

Fig. 1 The Business System Diamond

(Source: Hammer & Champey 1993)

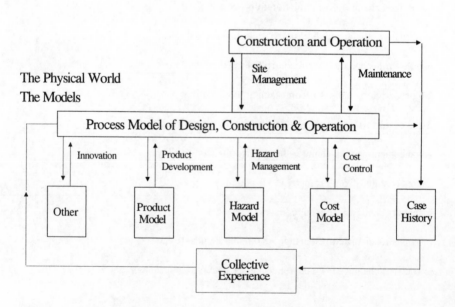

Fig. 2 Overview of Construction Process

Hammer and Champey's argument is that by re-engineering company processes ultimately everything changes because people, jobs, managers and values are linked together in a 'process diamond' (Fig 1).

IT and Process Modelling

At the root of re-engineering is IT. The power of new IT lies in thinking creatively about how it can be used. Hammer and Champey argue that the disruptive power of IT, (ie its ability to break the old rules that limit how we conduct our work) makes it critical to companies looking for the competitive advantage. For example through shared databases information can appear in as many places as needed. Business can reap the benefits of centralisation and decentralisation through telecommunications networks. Decision support tools can be made available to all and not just managers. Field personnel can send and receive messages wherever they happen to be through wireless data communication and portable computer. Automatic tracking technology can tell you where things are. Plans can get revised instantly rather than periodically.

Computer based process support systems which have within them models of company processes however require more research before they can be implemented within construction companies. In previous work the processes have generally been analysed in terms of activities (Platt, Blockley 1993). These processes have tended to be:

- pre-defined and contain relatively few decisions which depend on context,

- fairly linear and sequential,

- not concurrent or with very few concurrent activities,

- monitored and managed to ensure objectives are achieved,

- subject to little change over fairly long periods, and when change is made it is well controlled,

- time critical,

- typically high volume,

- fairly easily represented in terms of some form of work chart, such as a Role Activity Diagram (RAD), Data Flow Diagram (DFD) or IDEF0.

Studies of Quality Assurance in two civil engineering design offices have shown that the processes cannot easily be modelled in terms of tasks. It is impossible to capture all of the possible routes by which given objectives may be achieved. However, it was found that a relatively stable view of the processes could be obtained by focusing on responsibilities.

A process model role is therefore defined as a collection of responsibilities (Platt and Blockley 1993). Objectives are then translated into tasks to fulfil functions. A role is the proposed generic unit for both product and process models so that in a product model a role is a collection of functions. Products models describe artefacts with behaviour determined by

59

action and reaction. Process models describe human activity with action reaction and intentionality. Intentionality is the ability to represent the world to one's self purposefully. Thus a product role is a special restricted case of a process role (Dias, Blockley 1994).

A product role describes the functional design requirements. For example, a wall may have to bear loads, divide spaces, carry ducts, keep out weather and act as a thermal and acoustic barrier. A process role may also possess more than one responsibility, such as choosing structural form and design checking. A process role does not necessarily have to map into a single person in an organisational structure, since it can be inhabited, albeit in a limited sense, by a machine as well. Furthermore, a person or machine may inhabit more than one process role. Similarly, a given part of an artefact can have several product roles, which map onto the product components.

One significant advantage of this generic approach to modelling is that the above roles can be aggregated or decomposed recursively into other roles. For example, the product roles of "space", "room" and "floor" can be placed in increasing levels of an architectural system hierarchy. Process roles can also be defined at different levels of scope of responsibility or type; they can be, for example, technical, professional and managerial. A role at any given level in such a hierarchy will be a superset of the roles under it. Note that this is true for process roles only because they have been defined as collections of responsibilities and not as activities.

A process is modelled as a set of roles and interactions. A role is modelled by an interacting objecting (IO) which is a data structure built of software objects. The IO is a model of a piece of a system which interacts with other IOs to create system behaviour.

The principles behind the idea are that:-

-	complexity derives from interacting simplicity,

-	nature is parallel,

-	object oriented programming (OOP) is a suitable paradigm.

An IO is conceived as a holon after Koestler (1967) and described in a (set of) meta languages. It is discriminated from its environment at an appropriate level of definition and from an appropriate perspective in order to solve a problem. A holon is an entity which is both a part, and a whole. It is a part of a wider system (meta system) and is itself a system (of sub-systems). It exhibits emergent properties which result from the co-operation of its sub-systems (also holons). For example the capacity of a human being to walk and talk is a result of the co-operation of the sub-holons of the body such as the skeleton and nervous system etc each of which on their own do not have these properties. Similarly the corporate behaviour of a project team is undoubtedly influenced by the characteristics of its members, but also have a behaviour of its own, which emerges when the members are put together. The same is true of a structural frame (the whole) consisting of columns and beams (the parts).

Interactions occur by message passing between IOs. In an Interacting Objects Process Model (IOPM) (Chandra, Blockley, Woodman 1992) message input, processing and output in turn triggers input-processing-output sequences in other IO roles. In a process model, with human involvement, message input is filtered by perception, reflected upon (ie processed and involves intentionality) and then acted upon. This, in turn triggers perception-reflection- action sequences in other IO process troles sequences in other IO process roles.

Re-engineering the Construction Process

Fig 2 shows an overview of the construction process given that some form of model of the process is available (expressed in terms of roles and interactions). The traditional form of product model is the set of contract documents whereas future models may be entirely computer based. The safety and cost models are examples of specialised parts of the process management where particular forms of information are collected. Innovation often results from interactions with other disciplines and industries. Lessons can be fed through case histories into future process models to constitute a learning feedback loop.

However the most effective way to improve the safety performance of the construction company is to change the safety culture. The basic problem is the traditional view that safety and profitability are in direct conflict. This view is a product of the present culture of the industry. The thesis advanced here, but not yet tested, is that if companies use BPR principles, the ideas of 'practical learning' and the 3 Rs of hazard management then both safety and business profitability could be improved simultaneously.

Re-engineering for Safety

There are no established ways of examining construction industry processes for safety. In the process industry techniques such as HAZOP and HAZAN however are routinely used for examining the safety of the chemical production process.

The three Rs presented earlier are the basis of the approach but the focus is on understanding as **a set of processes not as a product**. *Remove* is the idea of designing for safety from the beginning - and it includes both the physical and organisational systems. *Reduce* is analogous to HAZOP where a design is examined by a team of engineers to try to identify what might happen and identify ways of redesigning the system as necessary. *Remedy* is the last stage of the process, analogous to HAZAN where protection systems are included if necessary. One of the central strategies of the nuclear industry for example is defence in depth where various protection systems are designed into the systems.

The Remove Option

Incubating hazards can be removed by an individual or team of engineers examining each sub-system and asking themselves particular questions. Sub-systems can be organisational eg the design team or physical eg a joint or member in a structure. The lists have here are not exhaustive and are given for illustration only. The question should be addressed periodically throughout the life of the project from scheme concept to decommissioning.

(i)   Is there evidence of 'incubating hazard' that can be removed such as

> inexperienced people being asked too much of them
> poor communications
> commonplace breaking safety rules
> wrong assumptions about emerging events
> poor information
> etc

(ii)   Are there physical system details that can be redesigned since they are not robust to variations in load/capacity/construction/operation

(eg in the sense that 'capacity' design' for earthquakes is robust)

> are not fail safe
> will fail in a brittle not ductile manner.
> have hidden critical member members that cannot be inspected
> are lacking in continuity
> are too sensitive to construction technique
> lack adequate strength or stiffness
> are too sensitive to changes in weather
> are too sensitive to failures in the immediate environs
> are sensitive to cyclic loading
> etc

The Reduce Option

After the remove option has been explored incubating hazards can be reduced by an individual or team of engineers examining each section of a system (eg a joint or member in a structure) at the detailed design stage in the manner of HAZOP and asking suitable "What if" questions. Certain key words may be developed eg what happens if more of, less of etc. The questions should also be addressed at period intervals throughout the life of the project. Again the lists are not exhaustive and are intended for illustration only.

Is there a particularly critical section of the system (sub-system)?

What happens if

(i)   the capacity (strength) of this section is degraded by

> some damage
> total damage

> eg   What happens if
> the joint moves
> a pin forms here
> the member (joint) fails
> stiffness is lost
> loads are shed

there is dilatation
swelling
shrinking
creep
a crack forms
there is water ingress
corrosion
erosion
maintenance is neglected
the contractor is inexperienced
the safety culture is poor
etc

(ii)   there is unusual demand (loading) through

repeated loads
sudden crowding with people
a sudden impact load
a load in different direction
a different erection sequence
an earthquake or other natural disaster (eg high wind)
dynamic resonance
extreme financial/political pressures
etc

(iii)   there is unusual usage of the section (operation) through

there is no competent person to maintain this section
a previously unanticipated usage
a section is cut out (hole etc)
etc

The Remedy Option

Incubating hazards can be reduced by an individual or team of engineers examining each
section of a system (eg a joint or member in a structure) at the detailed design stage and
during the life of the project in the manner HAZAN and asking suitable "What if" questions.

The remedy option is taken after the other two have been explored. Hazards are identified as
before. The emphasis however now is on attempting to predict likely consequences and to
estimate likelihoods (formally - probabilities of failure). Judgements about these however
must be made in context - that is why risk is defined above as the chance of occurrence plus
the consequences and the context. After re-design of detail the next consideration is to
consider protective sub-systems. For example fire protection is a standard way of protecting
steel beams and columns. In nuclear plant there is defence in depth through numerous
strategies and these are designed in a similar way to the main system since they themselves are
complex.

Conclusions

1. Good engineering requires quality. Quality is fitness for purpose. Safety is a part of quality.

2. At the root of safety is uncertainty is FIR (fuzziness, incompleteness or randomness). Uncertainty has to be managed and prediction is part of that process.

3. Failures generally incubate over time. The preconditions to failure are hazard.

4. The construction industry has a poor safety record which is probably due to a poor safety culture.

5. The ideas of Business Process Re-engineering could be used to change safety culture of the construction industry.

6. The three R' of hazard management are the remove, reduce and remedy options.

7. Techniques for evaluating the proneness to failure of a civil engineering system are being developed based on computer models of process.

8. Process modelling is based on the premise that roles and interactions are an effective way of describing what people do.

9. An Interacting Object (IO) has been defined as a data structure built of software objects. It represents a holon within a system which interacts with other IOs to create system behaviour. A holon is both a whole and a part.

10. A role has been proposed as a generic unit for both product and process models. A process role is a collection of responsibilities whereas a product role is a collection of functions. A function is a responsibility without intentionality.

References

ASCE (1988) Quality in the Constructed Project, Manual of Professional Practice, Vol 1, New York.

Bjork, B-C "Basic structure of a proposed building product model". Computer-Aided Design, Vol, 21, No 2 (March 1989) pp 71-78.

Blockley D I, "The Nature of Structural Design and Safety". England, Ellis Horwood Chichester UK, 1980.

Blockley D I (1992), "Engineering Safety", London, McGraw Hill, 1992

Butler B (1989) Safety First - Profits Last? Quality and Reliability Eng'g Int, Vol 5, 95 - 100.

CBI (1990) Developing a Safety Culture, London.

Chandra S, Blockley, DI and Woodman, NJ (1992) "An interacting objects physical process model". Computing Systems in Engineering, Vol 3, No 6, 661-670.

Coburn A and Spence R (1992) "Earthquake Protection", England John Wiley & Sons.

Comerford, JB and Blockley, DI (1993) "Managing safety and hazard through dependability". Structural Safety, Vol 12 (1993) pp 21-33.

Dester W, Blockley DI (1995) Safety - Behaviour and Culture in Construction, Eng'g Constr Arch Management, (in press).

Dias WPS, Blockley DI (1994) The Integration of Product and Process Models for Design, J Design Studies Vol 15 No 4 October, 417-432.

EERI Committee on Seismic Risk (1984) Glossary of Terms for Probabilistic Seismic-Risk and Hazard Analysis". *Earthquake Spectra*, Vol, 1, No 1, November 35-40.

Hammer M, Champey (1993) The Costs of Accidents at Work, HMSO, London.

Heiermann (1988) Increasing Safety Consciousness as an Employers Task, Gluehauf, Vol 124, No 3 Feb, 72-76, English translation, 141-144.

Koestler A (1967) The Ghost in the Machine, Hutchinson, London.

Pidgeon N F, Turner B a, Blockley DI, Toft B, (1991) Corporate Safety Culture: Improving the Management Contribution to System Reliability, Mathews RH (Ed), Proc Euro Reliability Conf, 682-690, Elsevier.

Platt D G, Blockley DI (1992): Analysis, Perception and Management, Report of Study Group, London.

Sanchez-Silva M, Taylor CA, Blockley DI (1994) "Proneness to Failure of Buildings in an Earthquake: A Systems Approach, 11th Euro Conf on Earthquake Eng. Vienna, Aug.

Steiner (1987) Assessing the Safety Climate of a Plant yields Long Term Benefits, Plant Eng'g Vol 14, No 8, April 23, 26-29

Wu X Blockley D I, Woodman N J "Structural Vulnerability Analysis Part I, Part II", Journal of Civ Eng. Systems, Vol 10, 301-333, 1993.

Turner B A (1978) Man Made Disasters, Wykeham Press, London.

Zadeh LA, (1975) Fuzzy Logic and Approximate Reasoning, Synthese, 30, 407-428.

A Methodology for Risk Management in Civil, Mechanical and Structural Engineering

M J BAKER[+], R J GRAVES[#] and M KEARNEY[*]

[+] Department of Engineering, University of Aberdeen, Aberdeen, Scotland, UK
[#] Department of Environmental & Occupational Medicine (DEOM), University of Aberdeen
[*] Formerly DEOM, University of Aberdeen, now with BAeSEMA, Aberdeen

ABSTRACT

The structured management of risk to employees and the general public lies at the heart of current UK health and safety legislation. It is only recently that formal approaches to risk assessment have been explicitly required; namely, with the introduction in 1992 of the Management of Health and Safety at Work Regulations and recently with the Construction Design and Management Regulations in 1995.

This paper highlights the steps taken to develop a prototype methodology for risk management in civil, mechanical and structural engineering (CMSE) activities. The work comprises a second phase of work commissioned by the Health and Safety Executive. The approach involved:

- development of a general risk management model associated with a CMSE project, and identification of the project stages and sub-systems which should be included;
- creation of a basic working model for sub-system risk management;
- a review of those hazard and risk assessment techniques identified in earlier work, and how these could be applied within CMSE; and,
- a desk-top application of the sub-system prototype risk management methodology to three selected case studies (cranes, falsework and trenching).

The approach makes use of a number of risk assessment techniques identified from earlier work, and has the anticipated benefits of providing financial savings through both improved system reliability and health and safety. Project planning is also seen to benefit from improved quality of information and improved and informed decision making throughout planning, design and operations stages.

The results from the desktop studies indicated that the sub-system risk management methodology should now be applied to construction projects to gauge its full effectiveness. On-site trials to be undertaken shortly will determine the areas needing refinement and development, and will assess the methodology's ability to reduce risk, and the resources required to do so. These trials will also determine the most effective way of monitoring, reviewing and maintaining such a risk management approach.

1. INTRODUCTION
1.1 Background
The management of risk to employees and the general public lies at the heart of current UK health and safety legislation[1], but it is only recently that formal approaches to risk assessment have been explicitly required; namely, with the introduction of regulations on the management of health and safety at work[2] in 1992 and more recently the Construction Design and Management (CDM) Regulations[3]. In some industries, even quantified risk assessment is now required for some activities – for example, for the survivability of offshore oil and gas installations[4] in UK waters.

The CDM regulations provide a milder form of control for the construction industry than that required onshore under the regulations[5] for major industrial hazards or offshore under the offshore installations safety case regulations[4], the main difference being that the latter require the production of formal safety cases.

Anyone doubting the practicability of providing a management system for the control of health and safety in construction should examine some of the safety cases now being submitted for offshore operations. These not only need to show that the risks have been assessed, but also to demonstrate ALARP – namely, that measures have or are being taken to reduce risks to a level which is as low as reasonably practicable, in a quantified way. Clearly it should be feasible to apply a similar quantified approach in the construction industry, but in a somewhat different way.

Earlier work[6] undertaken by the authors had reviewed literature and other information on the utility of risk assessment techniques in relation to Civil, Mechanical and Structural Engineering (CMSE) processes. This concluded that, "...*there had been little application of risk assessment techniques to the design, construction, normal use and maintenance phases of CMSE, but that there was considerable potential for the adaptation of techniques developed for other industries*".

1.2 The Need for Risk Management in the Construction Industry
The CDM regulations effectively allocate responsibilities for risk assessment to specific parties involved within a construction project, with particular reference to the client, planning supervisors, principal contractors and designers. It can be seen therefore that there is an emphasis at the planning and design phases of the construction project. This reflects an HSE view[7] that 90% of all fatalities within the construction industry could have been prevented, and that in 70% of cases, action by management could have saved lives. This is supported by the European Commission[8] which reported that 30% of all industrial fatalities within the European Community were in the construction industry, and went on to attribute the cause of 35% of site fatalities to designers, with a further 28% arising from communication problems between engineer/ architect and project contractor. It can be concluded from this that health and safety considerations at the project design and organisation phases have a direct bearing on approximately two-thirds of site accidents. Putting this into context, the accident statistics[9,10] for the British construction industry highlight some disturbing facts: 728 people were killed during the period 1981/2 to 1985/6; and 742 during 1986/7 to 1990/1 (see Figure 1). Taking the HSE view, over 1300 fatalities could have been prevented on British construction sites in the ten year period mentioned above, by the use of appropriate health and safety measures during the project design and organisation phases.

An HSE[7] report on the costs of accidents at work studied a construction site for eighteen weeks and proposed the accident ratio triangle shown in Figure 2. The findings at the end of the study showed that, statistically, for each reportable accident lasting over three days, there were over fifty-six minor injuries, and over three-and-a-half thousand non-injury accidents. There were no major injuries reported in the study.

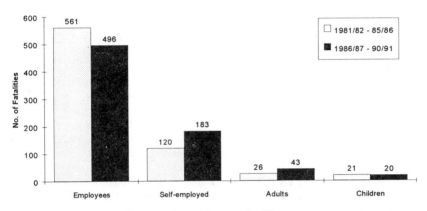

Fatalities in the Construction Industry

Note: 'Adults' and 'children' refer to members of the general public

Figure 1: Fatalities in the UK Construction Industry.

For the site studied, it was estimated that approximately £700,000 (8½%) worth of losses were incurred due to accidents, against its £8 million tender. This represents a substantial cost, and if representative of typical sites it highlights areas of opportunity where risk management can improve both health and safety, and provide economic benefits. It can be seen that a strong motivation for construction organisations to apply risk management principles would be the potential for savings from improved health and safety, with reduced costs from accidents and a reduction in the costs of achieving a given level of output.

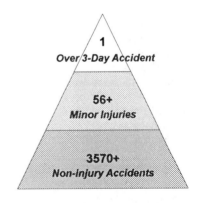

Figure 2: Accident Ratio Triangle

This paper describes recent work[11] to develop a practical methodology for risk management in CMSE. The aim has been to create a rigorous framework for risk management throughout the full life-cycle of a facility which allows the use of a range of qualitative and quantitative techniques, as appropriate.

2.   OVERVIEW OF RISK MANAGEMENT PRINCIPLES

Any discussion of risk requires a precise definition of terms, since many are not uniquely defined. The terms used in this paper largely follow HSE guidelines.

Within any form of risk assessment, the first step is to identify the physical hazards, namely those objects with the *potential* for causing harm – for example, a toxic or flammable or explosive substance, or objects with high potential or kinetic energy. Some physical hazards may be present for the complete life-cycle of the engineered facility (e.g. an active fault with the potential for causing an earthquake) whilst others (e.g. a deep excavation) may exist only during the construction phase, or during maintenance. Hence, an initial requirement is to sub-divide the life of the facility into a number of phases in order to identify where different types of hazard are likely to occur.

The phases will differ according to the type of system being considered, but for a civil engineering project these will be: site investigation, construction, commissioning, operating, any maintenance and repair phases, and finally the demolition phase. Clearly others also exist, such as the planning and design phases, but these are not times when physical accidents and failures can occur. It must be recognised however, that decisions are made in these earlier phases which can lead to failures and accidents in later phases.

The second step is to identify the possible accidents or failure modes associated with each hazard, or combinations of hazards, that could lead to the release of the hazard potential and then to determine the times in the life-cycle at which such events could occur. To be successful in finding the majority of these events requires the use of a systematic approach. This paper describes a modified form of so-called HAZOP[12,13] (hazard and operability) study approach which is suitable for this purpose.

Accidents, however, do not just happen and the third step is to study the possible range of triggering mechanisms, or conditions, which can give rise to each failure or accident. A number of examples are described below as the approach is developed. For some failures and accidents a combination or sequence of triggering conditions is needed, in other cases only one. In most accidents there is a final physical initiating event, for example the match or spark which set off the methane explosion at the Abbeystead valve house[14] in 1984. However, the final physical trigger is rarely the real cause of a failure or accident. The underlying causes, or the conditions which set the trigger, often relate back to earlier phases of the project, for example to the design or planning stages.

It is therefore necessary to work with at least three time frames in risk assessment – the time or times in the life of the project at which risk assessment is carried out, the times at which it is envisaged the failures or accidents can occur, and the times at which the underlying causes can originate.

The two remaining steps in risk assessment are the estimation of the probabilities or likelihoods that the necessary sequence of triggering events will occur for each particular hazard potential to be released, and an estimation of the consequences of each accident or failure. The latter may involve, fatalities, serious injuries, long-term health problems, environmental pollution and financial losses. For some accidents there may be more uncertainty in the magnitude of the consequences than in the likelihood of occurrence of the accident itself and vice-versa.

Risk management is, of course, much more than risk assessment. Typically it involves the steps described above, together with the introduction of control measures. The controls may be designed to work on the hazards themselves (e.g. it may be possible to eliminate or reduce them, once they have been identified), or on the triggering conditions, or on the magnitude of the potential consequences. In addition, risk management requires that there should be some form of ongoing audit to assess the effectiveness of the various measures taken and to provide the necessary feedback.

The scheme for risk management described below aims to show how the above can be applied in practice. In particular, it discusses the ways in which an engineering facility can be broken down into sub-systems and how the hazard identification technique can be used to examine situations at various stages in each sub-system's life.

3. THE DEVELOPMENT OF A METHODOLOGY FOR RISK MANAGEMENT
3.1 A Basic Working Model For Risk Management
The basic working model for risk management was created by integrating the concepts discussed in the Management of Health and Safety at Work Regulations 1992[2] with the concepts of risk assessment discussed in the previous work[6], and is illustrated in Figure 3.

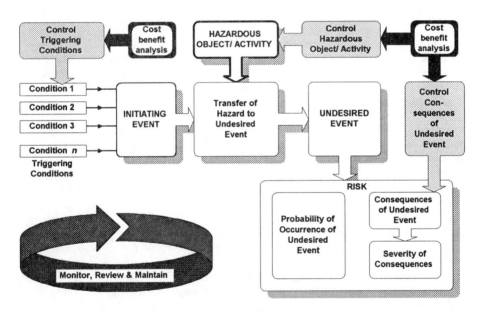

Figure 3: Basic Risk Management Model

The basic risk management model encompasses four key stages:

i) **hazard identification and evaluation**:
    This requires the identification of hazards – those activities/ objects which have the potential to cause damage, harm, injury or loss – and an evaluation of that potential.

ii)   **risk assessment**:
      This involves a number of steps
      - identification of the range of possible undesired events arising from the presence of each hazard
      - identification of the triggering conditions which could transfer the hazard potential into one or more undesired events
      - assessment of the likelihoods of the various undesired events
      - assessment of the respective consequences and their severity
      - evaluation of the risk (from knowledge of the likelihoods and consequences)

iii) **control of the hazard, triggering conditions and/ or consequences of the undesired event**:
      Once the spectrum of risks has been determined, the more significant risks can be targeted for control. This could involve: control of the hazards; control of the triggering conditions; and/ or control of the consequences arising from the undesired event.

      Control also introduces the concept of cost-benefit analysis[15], which aims to determine whether the final risk is acceptable or not; and if not, what resources are required to control the risk.

iv)   **monitor, review and maintain**:
      the final stage is to monitor, review and maintain the overall steps for hazard evaluation, risk assessment and the measures for control. The effectiveness of measures can be gauged by: tests and examinations; safety tours and inspections; occupational health surveys/ measurements; and safety audits.

Risk management can occur at different levels and stages in a construction project. The model shows that the process can be applied to hazardous objects, activities or a combination of these. For example, asbestos is a now well-documented hazardous substance (object), while the use of scaffolding is an example of a potentially hazardous activity. Clearly, there is a need to develop a practical methodology for identifying hazardous objects and activities as part of the risk assessment, control, and monitoring processes.

3.2   A Risk Management Methodology for Construction

As previously discussed, the phases in the life-cycle of a typical CMSE project at which accidents and failures can occur include: site investigation, construction, commissioning, operating, maintenance and repair, and finally decommissioning, demolition and removal. However, for the purposes of developing this risk assessment methodology, it is necessary to describe some broad categories of circumstances which can lead to accidents and failures. These should be read in conjunction with Figure 3.

i)   situations in which persons are injured as a result of direct exposure to a hazard without the occurrence of any physical engineering failure – e.g. as occurs through direct contact with an uninsulated high voltage cable, or through suffocation in a tunnel as a result of insufficient breathable air, or as a result of being struck by a moving object.

ii) situations in which a hazard can induce a physical failure which leads to undesired consequences (e.g. deaths, injuries and physical damage) resulting directly from that hazard – e.g. the failure of a dam as a result of being overtopped under extreme storm conditions leading to loss of the dam, the drowning of people downstream and physical damage to property.

iii) situations in which an Initiating Event can give rise to a physical failure, which in turn can release the potential of a further hazard – e.g. the presence of a defect in a weld in a vessel containing a toxic chemical, leading to fracture of the weld during routine handling and death or injury to people as a direct consequence of the release.

Given these situations, it is now necessary to introduce some new concepts for the purposes of risk assessment. To allow sub-division of the risk assessment process into manageable pieces of work, it is necessary to introduce the concepts of *Physical Sub-Systems* and *Operational Activities*.

For the purposes of this methodology, a Physical Sub-System is defined as a relatively self-contained part of either the permanent engineering facility being constructed, used or maintained, or some item of plant being used in a construction, maintenance or demolition process. Examples of the latter are cranes, compressors, welding equipment, etc. Examples of the former are: a building's foundations, a building's structural framework, a building's lift system, a powerstation turbine, etc.

The risk management of these sub-systems is therefore a major part of overall project risk management. In effect, the results of the risk assessments of sub-systems provide the components to enable risk assessors to control overall risk.

An Operational Activity in a CMSE project is defined as a process relating to the use of one or more physical sub-systems, at some time during its life. Examples of this are: the erection of a tower crane, the erection of part of a building structure using the range of necessary equipment, creating an excavation, installing scaffolding, etc.

Figure 4 shows the composition of a Physical Sub-system and how it interacts with an Operational Activity (Sub-system User Application). Examination of the design and production stages the sub-system, and subsequent operational stages, shows that there are two basic groups of people associated with it:

i) the sub-system producer, encompassing planners, designers, manufacturers and suppliers of the sub-system; and,

ii) the sub-system user, who could be anyone who has an interest in the application of the sub-system for CMSE projects, including the client, construction planners, designers/ architects, engineers, contractors and/ or operatives. Note that the sub-system producer and sub-system user may be one-and-the same.

Ideally the sub-system *producer* is responsible for the design specification of his sub-system, and should produce both a physical profile and a specification of operational intent for the sub-system. This expands on the theme of '*suitability of work equipment*' as specified in the guidance on work equipment[16]. The sub-system *user* would then be able to use the information passed on from the producer's physical profile and/or operational specification to create a method statement giving the user's operational intent for the sub-system. This corresponds to the proposals for the supply and access to information on health and safety throughout a project's life, as proposed in the health and safety plan and file of the CDM Regulations.

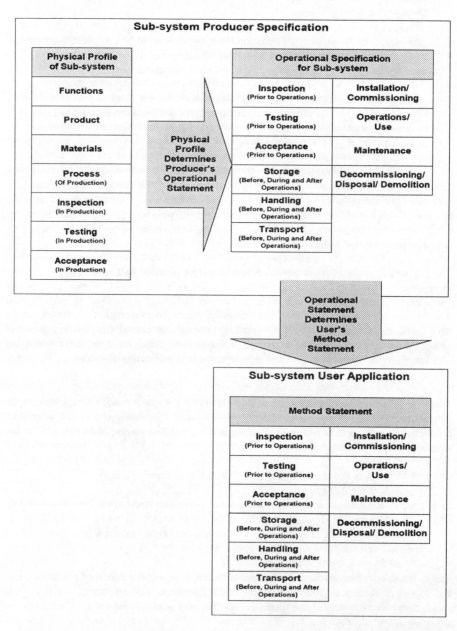

Figure 4:   Physical Sub-system in relation to an Operational Activity of a CMSE project

Figure 5 illustrates the proposal for the flow of information between sub-system producer and user throughout a sub-system's life. The feed-through of information in the form of the proposed health and safety documentation is complemented by feed-back to the sub-system producer of physical and/ or operational failings in order that he may take measures to control these.

From the above it can be seen that there are three issues relating to the risk management of the different phases of CMSE projects, (see Figure 5):

i)   there is the need for an assessment of the activities to be carried out at the planning, design and production (manufacturing) stages of each sub-system, questioning if the sub-system and its component parts are suitable for the functions they are to perform. This assessment should question the *producer's* function, product and material specifications at the planning and design stages. There are also questions relating to the production process(es) for the sub-system, asking if these can assure the eventual reliability of the sub-system and its component parts. These should query whether the manufacturing processes, testing, inspection and acceptance specifications for each item are appropriate.

ii)   there is the need for an assessment of each sub-system *user's* method statement in order to assess his/her intended use of the sub-system, when compared with the sub-system producer's ideal operational specification; and,

iii)   there is the need for an assessment of each sub-system user's on-site practices, when compared with his/her intentions as specified in the method statement.

These issues are recognised in BS 5750[17], where the need to control design in order to meet specific product requirements, including reliability, means an examination of procedures for each stage of a product's life. It is also clear that the risk management of different phases of CMSE projects should not only address the physical sub-systems and their components, but also the actions of CMSE personnel, and their interaction with each sub-system.

Whilst it may appear that conducting this number of assessments would be resource intensive, it is clear that the work would be shared among a number of groups. Furthermore, for the sub-system user, much of the work would already have been done by the sub-system producer, and the user would only have to adapt the producer's assessments for his/her purposes. The most cost effective way forward for the user, is for generic assessments to be prepared which would be supplemented by on-site assessments of the practices actually undertaken.

This approach is somewhat similar to that required by the regulations for the control of hazardous substances[18].

In conclusion, it is suggested that the prototype risk management methodology:
- should be sub-system oriented; and,
- should examine the stages within each sub-system's life, from conception right through to disposal, in order to evaluate the hazards and risks associated with its physical profile and operational characteristics.

The remainder of this paper concentrates on the development of a practical risk assessment methodology for Physical Sub-systems.

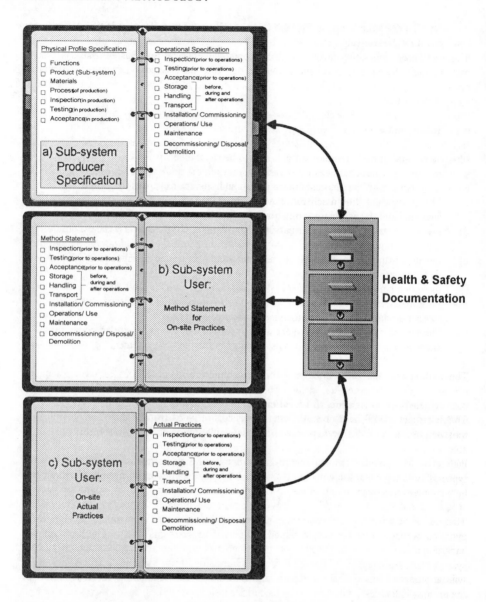

Figure 5: Flow of Information Between Sub-system Producer and User

4.   DEVELOPMENT OF A PRACTICAL SUB-SYSTEM RISK ASSESSMENT METHODOLOGY

This section describes the development of a practical Physical Sub-System risk assessment methodology, being a component of the wider risk management of entire engineering systems. In particular, it explores how it is anticipated a user will carry out the practical steps in the process.

4.1   Basic requirements

It is clear that an ideal Physical Sub-System based risk assessment methodology should satisfy a number of basic requirements. It should be capable of:

a)   identifying significant hazards at various stages in the sub-system's life;

b)   identifying both the physical failure modes and operational undesired events;

c)   identifying the failure mechanisms which could lead to a release of each hazard's potential and the associated triggering conditions;

d)   assessing the nature and severity of the consequences of each type of physical failure and other undesired events;

e)   enabling estimates to be made of the likelihood of each type of physical failure and other undesired events;

f)   assessing the resulting risks;

g)   determining the control measures which could reduce the likelihood of undesired events and mitigate their consequences; and finally

h)   allowing the interactions between various sub-systems to be taken into account and their influence evaluated.

The methodology has been developed with these requirements in mind.

4.2   Hazard Identification and Evaluation

The first stage which the user must undertake is hazard identification, and this is perhaps the most important, as it is this stage which focuses attention on the path to be followed to be able to identify relevant initiating events. Failure to identify hazards will result in an ineffective assessment. Once a hazard has been identified it is much easier to visualise the types of initiating event which could be relevant to that hazard. In most situations, there will be a number of hazards to consider.

The next step is hazard evaluation which is the process involved in mapping each initiating event to the triggering conditions which could lead to such an event. It is proposed that hazard evaluation for both the physical characteristics and operational practices of the sub-system could be achieved by the application of a modified form of HAZOP technique, which will be referred to as HAZID (HAZard IDentification). This latter term is currently used in the process industries in the context of hazard identification studies, and is therefore not new. The same word is used here to avoid the proliferation of terms, but recognising that there are likely to be a number of differences in approach. This process generates much of the data used in subsequent stages.

Earlier, in Figure 3, it was seen that one or more conditions could lead to an Initiating Event, which in turn could lead to some Undesired Event – a physical failure or other accident. This transforms the Hazard into an Undesired Event. This concept is illustrated in more detail in Figure 6 which shows how the deviations in one or more important property of a component can result in such an Initiating Event. Clearly, being able to list the critical properties and possible deviations for components of a sub-system that lead to an Initiating Event provides a means of identifying them, and then controlling their escalation, and hence preventing the transfer of Hazard potential.

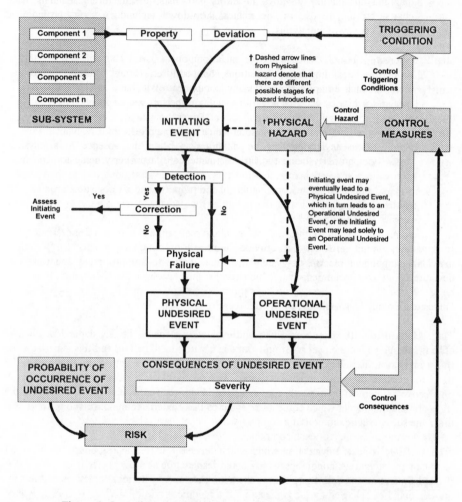

Figure 6: Overall Model Of Sub-system Risk Management Approach

In practice a group of experts would use each Hazard as a starting point to generate a HAZID vocabulary (see below) to determine, from possible Initiating Events, those which could lead to an Undesired Event. These events may have either a technical or human origin. The intention is that the HAZID process is used at the planning and design stages by the sub-system producer, aiding him/her in assessing the suitability of the sub-system for the purpose for which it is intended.

The HAZID process has the following steps in identifying triggering conditions within the chosen construction sub-system:

Step 1: To generate a list of the component parts of the sub-system by using detailed, documented descriptions of the sub-system in question: piping and/ or instrumentation diagrams; schematics, block diagrams, logic diagrams; process flow diagrams; installation drawings; inventory parts lists; manufacturers' manuals; flow charts, etc. The use of hierarchical, top-down techniques could provide an illustrative way of aiding this.

Step 2: To create a HAZID vocabulary for each component part. This will define relevant properties (e.g. dimensions, positions, temperatures, forces, material properties, etc.) for each component. As many components will have similar properties, a general list may be used for all, with specific properties being appended as required.

Step 3: To determine the extreme deviations which might apply to each relevant property. The extreme deviations may be classified as being the absence of a physical property; a property being too little or inadequate; a property being too much or excessive; a property being outwith limits or being adverse; and/ or a property being wrongly specified. The combination of the property and its deviation produces an Initiating Event, which has the potential for damage, harm, injury or loss, when applied to the Hazard.

In summary, the HAZID process provides a means of compiling a checklist for each individual component of the sub-system and attributing relevant properties and potential deviations (of those properties) to it. The checklist thus enables a list of Initiating Events to be generated, be they physical or operational, which have the potential to realise an Undesired Event. This is illustrated in Figure 6.

The success of the hazard identification and evaluation stages is largely dependent on five criteria:
i) the identification of the appropriate hazards;
ii) the comprehensive identification of those components which make up the overall sub-system (internal components, e.g. couplers, tubing, etc. in the case of scaffolding), and those components which come into contact with it (external components, e.g. soil);
iii) the successful generation of a comprehensive vocabulary which can describe the relevant properties for each component;
iv) the ability to determine the extent to which deviations in relevant properties are important, and whether these take factors of safety into account; and,
v) the qualifications and experience of the expert members who make up the HAZID group.

The application of the HAZID technique requires experienced personnel. In the process industries, the time taken to complete typical HAZOPs range from several days to weeks, depending upon the complexity of the system. For construction projects, it is envisaged that HAZID's might take a similar length of time.

4.3 Risk Assessment

Risk assessment is the second stage of the prototype sub-system risk management methodology. This stage should be conducted both by the sub-system producer at the sub-system planning and design stages, and the sub-system user prior to, and during, operations.

The first step of the risk assessment procedure is to determine the range of possible undesired events arising from initiating events identified by the HAZID process.

Undesired Events. All undesired events can be grouped into one of two categories, termed here as physical undesired events and operational undesired events, as shown in Figure 6. An operational undesired event is defined as an event leading to death or injury, or a near-miss, in which there is no physical failure of any part of the system (e.g. a person being struck by a moving object, or a fall from a height). A physical undesired event, on the other hand does involve some degree of physical failure, for example, as a result of wear or corrosion of part of a sub-system during use. The latter may, or may not, lead on to an operational undesired event.

Figure 7a illustrates an operational undesired event. In this example, the physical hazard is the kinetic energy of an item being moved by a crane, but the cause of the operational undesired event is a deviation from the operator's system of correct procedures.

Figure 7b illustrates circumstances in which there are both physical and operational undesired events. Here, the initiating event is a component which has been incorrectly manufactured. The principle hazard is the potential energy in the object being lifted, which because of the presence of the initiating event leads to fatigue and then to physical failure of the crane. This physical failure of the crane may then lead to an operational undesired event, the death and injury of people. It should be noted that in this example, the principal hazard is not associated with the initiating event. It some situations, however, it may be.

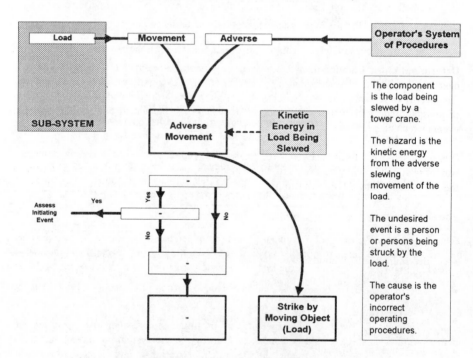

Figure 7a Operational undesired event

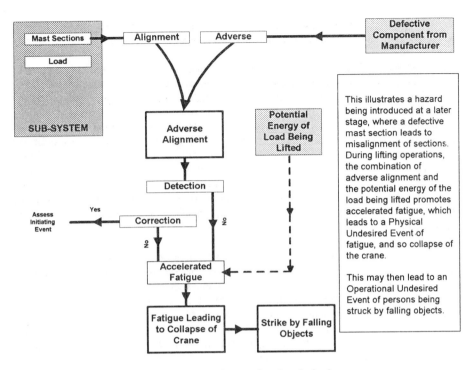

Figure 7b Physical and operational undesired events

Determination of Likelihood of Undesired Events and Severity of Consequences. The next step requires a determination of the likelihood of each significant undesired event and the severity of its consequences. Success is dependent upon the comprehensive identification of possible undesired events, and knowing how these can be related back to the initiating events which caused them.

It is proposed that a form of Event Tree Analysis[19,20] should be used to provide a systematic way of relating the initiating events to the final consequences. The results can then be used in the next stage of the risk assessment to provide measures of both financial and personnel risk.

The steps are as follows:
- select a property deviation of a component which may finally lead to the undesired event;
- determine the likelihood that the initiating event will de detected, before serious damage can occur;
- determine the corresponding likelihood of recovery from, or correction of, the initiating event;
- assess the likelihood that the initiating event will escalate to give rise to an undesired event; and finally,
- determine the consequences of the undesired event, and their severity.

Since data on the frequencies of these types of event are unlikely to be available in most situations, it is proposed that the various likelihoods are obtained by expert judgement using specially selected teams of experts, for example as convened in the process industries for HAZOP studies. Techniques such as absolute probability judgement and the method of paired comparisons can then be used to rank the likelihoods of different scenarios and to test the consistency of the various 'experts' employed on the task.

For the evaluation of risk, the consequences of all significant undesired events also need to be assessed. The severity of the consequences can be expressed in financial terms for the physical damage that may occur and in terms of injury/harm to people for the operational undesired events. These two components may be kept separate or it may be appropriate to express the latter in financial terms using appropriate data from former compensation claims. It should be stressed that in all cases it is appropriate in the subsequent decision-making process to explore the sensitivity of the results to a range of assumptions about the financial cost of human accidents.

Determination of the Risk. The last stage in this process is to evaluate the resulting risk from a knowledge of the consequences and their likelihoods. This may be done by associating a consequence and a likelihood with every branch of each event tree. The product of these for each branch is then a component of the total risk, and the total risk is obtained by summing over all the possible outcomes.

The use of the results obtained depend on whether the risk assessment is being undertaken by the sub-system producer or the sub-system user. In any case, it is proposed that the sub-system user will take the information from the producer and will use it to assist in his/ her own assessment.

4.5   Control Measures
When the most significant risks have been determined, the next stage of the methodology requires that the underlying causes should be targeted for control. This re-introduces the idea of triggering conditions, as shown in Figure 3. The classification of triggering conditions involves consideration of performance shaping factors and human error modes, as discussed in the literature on human reliability analysis (for example see references 21-24).

It is considered that each possible triggering condition leading to an undesired event can be attributed to a stage of design, construction, or maintenance and this indicates whether it is the producer or user of the sub-system who is failing in their duties.

Finally, remedial action should be specified, indicating how the undesired events and their effects can be controlled. This involves a hierarchy of control measures, with these being applied not only to the cause of the initiating event and triggering conditions, but also to the hazards and the consequences of failure (Figure 6).

5.   CONCLUSIONS FROM DESKTOP APPLICATION OF METHODOLOGY
The prototype methodology described above was applied to three CMSE sub-systems – a tower crane, a falsework sub-system and a trenching support sub-system. The work allowed the researchers to investigate the feasibility of applying the methodology. Examples of the HAZID documentation are presented in the main report[11], together with the mechanics of the

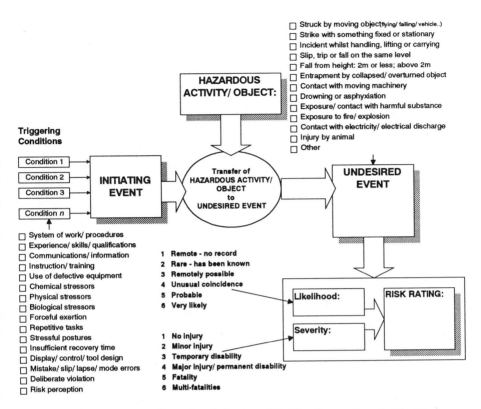

Figure 8: Worksheet illustrating derivation of likelihood, severity and risk rating

overall process. For the study, different types of recording sheet or proforma were developed, but are not included here for lack of space. However, Figure 8 illustrates the general procedure and Table 1 gives the approach for determining the risk rating.

The main conclusions reached were as follows:

(1) The prototype methodology provides an approach which could be used for risk management in CMSE, but not without additional resources; there may, however, be additional benefits.

(2) Acquisition of data requires the support of sub-system producers/ suppliers and users.

(3) The involvement of various expert groups (HAZID groups) is necessary.

(4) The approach is likely to need on-site assessments to supplement desk-top studies.

(5) Even without accurate likelihood values, the methodology provides a means whereby hazards and their consequences can be determined, and control measures and stages for control can be assessed.

(6) With a shortage of likelihood values, the absolute significance of risks cannot be determined, which means the decision making is less precise for the targeting of control measures.

Rating:	LIKELIHOOD	SEVERITY	RISK RATING
	Considering the hazardous activity/ object & possible triggering conditions, and the possible frequency, duration and level of exposure and population exposed, then the likelihood of the undesired event being realized is:	If the undesired event is realized, the severity of the consequences is likely to be:	Likelihood rating x Severity rating
1	remote (no recorded cases)	remote (no recorded cases)	
2	rare (has been known)	minor injury	
3	remotely possible	major injury (1): temporary disablement	
4	unusual coincidence	major injury (2): permanent disablement	
5	probable	fatality	
6	very likely	multiple fatalities	

Table 1: Example of simple generation of risk rating

(7) Applying the methodology can provide a set of best practice procedures, which should aid project management, and, by users questioning practices at an early stage, can avoid costly action at a later date.

(8) Field trials are needed to assess the acceptability of the proposed risk management methodology.

(9) The development of databases on component failures and human errors for CMSE sub-systems and operations is likely to incur some additional costs. Some data may, however be available from each organisation's day-to-day operations.

(10) Incorporating risk assessment techniques within the prototype sub-system risk management methodology provides a means of:
- identifying initiating events which could lead to physical and/ or operational undesired events
- using the initiating events to determine the consequential effects of undesired events, and determine the significance of the risk of these
- using the significance of risk to make decisions on where to target control measures to the initiating event and its associated triggering conditions, or to the consequences of the undesired events.

(11) The additional benefits of applying the prototype sub-system risk management methodology for CMSE projects are expected to be:
- Improved quality of information, informed decision making, with improved project planning, through the sharing of health and safety documentation for planners, designers, manufacturers, architects, engineers, contractors, etc.

- Financial savings associated with the prevention/ reduction of accidents on-site. with anticipated savings in the reduction of: lost time due to the loss of personnel; cost of downtime and work stoppages; cost of replacement labour and training; medical treatment and compensation; plant and equipment damage; cost of repairs/ replacement/ rework; environmental damage; and possibly reduced insurance premiums
- The potential for quality improvements at sub-system design and production stages, through questioning design specifications.

REFERENCES

1. Health and Safety Commission (1992). *A guide to the health and safety at work etc. Act 1974*. London: HMSO.
2. Health and Safety Commission (1992). *Management of health and safety at work 1992 – Approved code of practice*. London: HMSO.
3. Health and Safety Commission (1994). *Managing construction for health and safety - Draft approved code of practice*.
4. Great Britain (1992). *Offshore installations (safety case) Regulations 1992*.
5. Great Britain (1984). *The control of industrial major accident hazards Regulations 1984*. SI 1902.
6. Baker M J and Finlayson M (1993). Review of literature and other information on the utility of risk assessment techniques in relation to construction processes. Aberdeen University. Report to the Health and Safety Executive, HSE Contract: RSU 3088/R35,43.
7. Health and Safety Executive. (1993). *The costs of accidents at work*. London: HMSO.
8. New Civil Engineer (18 Feb. 1993). *Design causes 35% of European site deaths*.
9. Health and Safety Executive (1988). *Blackspot construction - a study of five year fatal accidents in the building and civil engineering industries*. London: HMSO.
10. Health and Safety Commission (1991). *Annual report - 1990/ 91*. London: HMSO.
11. Kearney M, Baker M J and Graves R J (1994). Development of a prototype risk management methodology. Report to the Health and Executive on a pilot investigation of the use of risk assessment techniques in certain aspects of civil, mechanical and structural engineering. University of Aberdeen, Department of Engineering.
12. Chemical Industries Association (1977). *HAZOP – A Guide to Hazard and Operability Studies*.
13. Kletz T (1992). *HAZOP and HAZAN . Identifying and Assessing Process Industry Hazards*. Institution of Chemical Engineers, (3rd edition).
14. Methane Safety Guide Follows Abbeystead (1984). *New Civil Engineer*, 5 July 1984, p 4-5.
15. Bamber L. (1990). Risk management: techniques and practices. In: *Safety at work*. Third edition, Butterworth-Heinemann Ltd.
16. Health and Safety Executive (1992). *Work equipment - provision and use of work equipment regulations 1992 - guidance on regulations*. London: HMSO.
17. British Standards Institution (1990). *BS 5750: Part 1 - specification for design/ development, production, installation and servicing*.
18. Great Britain (1988). *The control of substances hazardous to health regulations 1988*. SI 1657.
19. Thomson JR (1987). *Engineering safety assessment - an introduction*. Longman Scientific and Technical.

20. Sundararajan, C (Raj) (1991). *Guide to reliability engineering - data, analysis, applications, implementation, and management*. Van Nostrand Reinhold.
21. Reason, James. (1990). *Human error*. Cambridge: Cambridge University Press.
22. Wickens, Christopher D (1992). *Engineering psychology and human performance - second edition*. Harper Collins.
23. Rasmussen J, Duncan K and Leplat J (eds) (1987). *New technology and human error*. John Wiley and Sons.
24. Kirwan, Barry (1994). *A guide to practical human reliability assessment*. Taylor and Francis.

Ambition Control

Mr P GODFREY, Sir William Halcrow

INTRODUCTION

This brief paper has been introduced to provide delegates with some holistic concepts that have helped the author to relate some of the systematic risk control methods adopted in the chemical and defence industries to use in the "infrastructure" industry. In providing and maintaining infrastructure, we are often faced with high levels of uncertainty with many prototype constructions. We seldom have the opportunity to test our designs to destruction in practice. We are inevitably in direct contact with the public who are often the prime users of the facilities we create.

Understanding what people want and need is at the root of the design process. The contribution of social scientist, psychologists and marketeers can be beneficial in this process and promote practical improvements in safety management. Indeed "human factors" may be regarded as the key issue.

Good risk control has been evolved, from experience, by most successful owners who have had the time and stability to do so. However, as the pace of change accelerates and public expectations rise through prosperity to demand higher levels of safety, so the need to improve our methods of risk control increases. Systematic methods endeavour to make the risks explicit so that they can be more effectively controlled. Use of the methods is not restricted to safety issues. This is helpful as it will allow the strong connection that exists between good safety and sound business management practice to overcome the misconception among many that safety is a cost rather than a benefit. With this in mind Figure 1 "Control of Ambitions" is introduced as a simple safety marketing model which recognises that all ambitions have an up and a down side to them. It is further suggested that normally owners will be more ambitious where there is confidence that the business is under sound control. Thus control is regarded as a prime mover rather than an inhibitor of effective action.

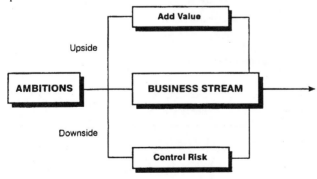

Figure 1 Control of ambitions

INCLUDING CREATIVE PROCESSES

It is all too easy to adopt a simple actuarial approach to the management of risk. The very issues that are encouraging the development of systematic methods, such as cultural, organisational and technological change or novelty, are those that cannot be controlled by simple extrapolations from the past. They require additional techniques aimed at using understanding of behaviour, to design for the future.

In practice, like engineering itself, risk control is a creative process that is aimed at improving the future rather than just accounting for the past. Learning lessons from the past are an essential but not sufficient part of the process. The extra element is described as "creativity". Table 1 compares creative processes with lesson learning ones.

Creative	Learning from the past
Foresight	Hindsight
Forecasting	Accountancy
Planning	History
Design	Audit
Investment	Valuation
Prevention	Investigation

Table 1   Creative and learning processes

The inclusion of creative processes into the simple marketing model introduces the concepts of value and risk potentials as shown in Figure 2, "Creative Control of Ambitions":

- Problems, hazards and threats have potential for harm
- Opportunities have potential for adding value

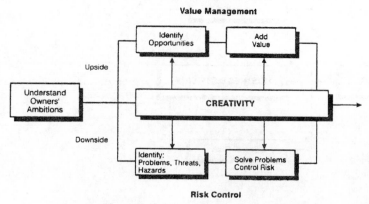

Figure 2 Creative control of ambitions

CASE EXAMPLE

Figure 3 applies the creative model to an infrastructure owner, eg a transportation company, whose ambition is to generate continuous improvement in cost, safety, environment and quality through his projects.

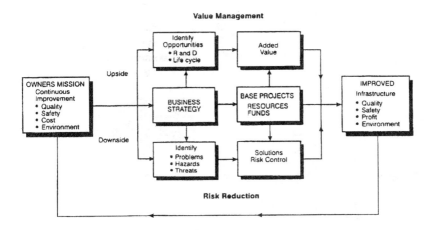

Figure 3 Case example infrastructure owner

CONTROL PROCESS

When looked at systematically control or risk and management of value are similar processes in terms of what needs to be done. The need in each case is to:

- identify
- assess
- plan action for control
- consider cost benefit
- consider who owns the actions and the outcomes
- decide what to do.

Figure 4 provides a simple method of controlling risk and value derived from extending the basic method described in the "Control of Risk"[7] document being prepared by Halcrow and others for CIRIA. To this has been added the "bones" of the value management process. The criteria for tolerability and acceptability of investment and risks depend on the nature of the outcomes. For example, investment in safety provisions will be subject to different criteria from an investment that simply increases turnover. Never-the-less we have been using these principles in safety risk assessments and have found that by preparing the models on the same map we have been able to demonstrate opportunities that arise from safety mitigation measures that would not have been otherwise appreciated. The outcome is a greater commitment to employment of cost beneficial safety measures.

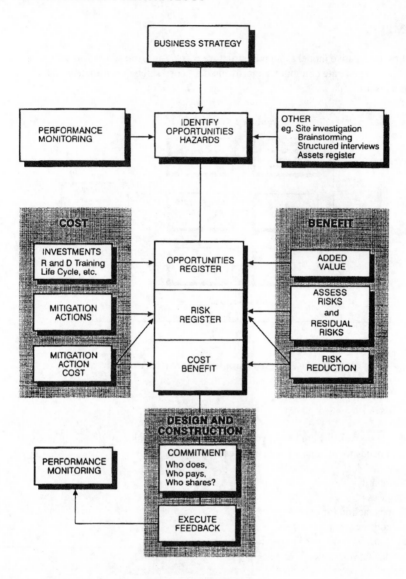

Figure 4 Risk and value control

CONCLUSION

The best risk mitigation measures improve performance, add value and increase safety.

A lot of beneficial safety measures can be ruled out if considered in isolation. Simultaneous safety, value and risk management will allow the full benefit of systematic methods to be realised collectively.

This paper presents a concept, which it is hoped will stimulate creative ideas.

REFERENCES

1. Engineering Council; Code of Professional Practice on Engineers and Risk Issues; 1992.

2. The Engineering Council, Guidelines on Risk Issues; ISBN 0-9516611-7-5; 1993.

3. M Latham, Constructing The Team, Final Report of the Government/Industry Review of Procurement and Contractual Arrangements in the Construction Industry; 1994, ISBN 0-11-752994-X.

4. European Construction Institute, Total project management of construction safety, health and environment; Thomas Telford, ISBN 0 7277 1923 8. 1992.

5. HSE, The Tolerability of Risk from Nuclear Power Stations, HMSO, 1992, ISBN 0118863681.

6. J D Rimmington CB, Coping with Technological Risk: A 21st Century Problem. Royal Academy of Engineering. 1993.

7. Godfrey P S; "The Control of Risk"; Seventh Annual Conference on Risk, Management & Procurement in Construction; Organised by The Centre of Construction Law & Management, King's College London; September 1994.

8. P S Godfrey; The Holistic Approach; Coping with Complexity in Procurement; Institution of Mechanical Engineers Railway Division; 1993.

9. P S Godfrey; The Holistic Approach to Risk Engineering in the Construction Industry, Safety and Reliability Society Conference Manchester, 1993.

SESSION 2 : The discussion

Professor D.Blockley   Process re-engineering for safety.

Professor M.J.Baker   A Methodology for Risk Management in Civil,
                            Mechanical and Structural Engineering.

P.Godfrey   Ambition Control - from the floor

E Hambly
You talked about multiple causes and trigger events. One conclusion I've drawn from the
number of situations that have multiple causes is to draw the conclusion that everything we
look at has got one thing wrong with it. It only takes a second fault and we have a problem so
that in a way you can have it without multiple causes.

D.Blockley, University of Bristol.
There are some very famous accidents have occurred from just a single cause. I can think of a
major bridge that collapsed just because someone calculated the average shear stress by taking
the complete cross sectional area of the steel beam instead of just the web area, which of
course we know we should do, the bridge failed just because of that mistake. That is relatively
rare, normally it is a complex problem.

B.Finney, Sir William Halcrow and partners.
I agree with everything you have said with one exception. I would place safety as part of
management and not quality, there is a financial side to it.

D.Blockley
I agree and disagree. Surely, if you are running an effective company, quality is just fitness for
purpose. If the company is not making any money it is not fit for its purpose because it is not
going to be successful. I think we are not disagreeing, it is about management, management is
about quality depending upon what you define the purpose of the company is.

R.Owen,HSE.
I don't wish to put a question, simply a statement of support concerning the last slide that you
showed about the collective experience of the industry. I'm currently investigating the collapse
at Heathrow. As a result of that we are looking in some detail at experience on tunnel
collapses on a world basis. There is little collective experience available. The ability to learn
from other people's mistakes is a very valuable process in terms of management of risk. It is
very difficult to embark upon the process of risk assessment if you don't have some
understanding of what sort of failures have already occurred. I just wonder, as an example,
how many people in this room have ever or would be prepared to now actually stand up and
give us a lecture on something that they have failed to achieve satisfactorily, as an illustration
of examples of failure. I see from the reaction that the general perception, which I know to
be true, is that we are all very reluctant to talk about failures. It is only by changing that
culture and actually talking about what has gone wrong and what we have now done to put it

right, that we will actually collectively learn from that experience. If this conference can get that process entrained it will have been very worthwhile indeed.

D.Blockley
I talked about my banana skin manager, one of the rules about banana skin management is to see failures and opportunities to learn.

E.Dore, Standing Comittee on Structural Safety.
As many people will know the Standing Committee on Structural Safety has a brief to foresee the future in a sense that it has to look at trends and identify them publically, before other people have met the problem.

Professor Blockley said that a lot of information is not coming back to us because of proprietary inhibitions and the last speaker mentioned the inhibitions that are natural to all of us. We have been trying to stimulate the industry or the profession to come clean, in a sense, and to report the near misses that are occurring all of the time, perhaps to a minor extent, but which, if magnified as they can be, will become serious and will together provide evidence statisitically.

I think Professor Blockley mentioned the contribution which information technology can make, would it be as support to a central collector of information which would include case histories of failure and case histories of these near misses, which could be totally confidential.

D.Blockley
I totally support that. Perhaps we can get some sort of semi-formalised process, through the Standing Committe and maybe through the Institutions, by which people are encouraged to report near misses, as they are in other industries such as the aircraft industry - pilots are encouraged to report on near misses and so on, anonymously if necessary. If we could get feed-back of that sort it would be an enormous contribution.

John Dawson, Rendel,Palmer and Tritton.
It seems to me that if you have a big project, £100 million or so, the problem of doing a risk assessment is fairly easy. If it is a £1000 million project it is easier still. If I were asked to manage such a project I would know exactly what I needed to do and how I would go about it, with the help of advisers. I put it to this meeting that the really tough projects are those that have a capital value of around £1 million. I really haven't heard much today regarding advice I can give my colleagues on what we practically do on these smaller projects. Without trying to answer my own question I would like to put some pointers in the direction we might go.

What I would like to know is how we blend together these first principles evaluations which we do, and which I have some experience of, with the more practical approach. The historical approach of the industry has been to take risk much more generically. We say this is a process, eg, a lifting operation, and somebody somewhere has written some guide of good practice which sets down a safe way of doing it and we just do it. Somehow our methodologies should address more than the question of quantification and the first principles aspect. We have really got to work towards melding together conventional industry good practice with first principles appraisals.

J.Mather, W.S.Atkins.

I would like to say that small construction sites can probably be looked at in the same way as one of the subsystems I was looking at. Providing the contractor is able to develop a generic procedure for working on small sites, then this is the way forward. It is better than relying on people who are on site to do that risk assessment, but they should, obviously, be aware of the results of it and the restrictions that it places on them. I would agree this is a major problem in practice because of the large porportion of work that is carried out is of a small capital value.

E Hambly

I believe this is a situation where management and safety run hand in hand. I see the method statement that a contractor produces to describe how he is going to go about the job as, fundamentally, a risk assessment process. If you wished to paint this room the method statement you would produce would be a visualisation of risks and be a risk assessment. This is why the CDM regulations place much importance on having a clear description of the job.

P.Brand, AEA Technology.

There is an interesting risk management system presently being put in at AWE Aldermaston. Professor Baker may be able to obtain some of the details through the offices of the HSE. I believe it deals with some of the concerns that have been expressed. It is trying to address the localised small level risks and obtain information from the people who are actually at risk from the smaller level projects.

The main point I wished to make was to support the act of piracy of Mr.Godfrey. This idea of looking at hazards and safety means we should also be looking at opportunity. The Chairman commented earlier that safety will save us money some day, but we are still looking for an example. Part of the answer to that is that the value of looking at safety and of looking at hazard is the process itself. I do have an example.

I was involved in a project recently, where we were looking at project risk so we were looking at time and cost scheduling as wel, as safety with regard to a chemical processing contract. A number of the results that came out suggested that what was required, in order to improve the hazard situation both in terms of the project and safety, was to change the entire contract strategy. To change the risk transfer between the two parties involved, in fact there was a third party. The change in the contract strategy lead to the expectation of increased profit of £1 - £1.5million on a £30 million pound contract.

P.Wigley, Railtrack plc.

I am responsible for providing a set of safety standards that relate to Railtrack's infrastructure. There are a couple of points I would like to make that might be helpful here. A key to this is to have a systematic approach. The Health and Safety guidelines are very useful in that you need to create a policy, and an organisation to implement and monitor it.

Each of the standards we are providing is, in itself, a miniature safety management system. In designing a suite of standards to cover the whole life costs of a bridge from design to maintenance, renewal and decommissioning, it has been useful for me to consider an electrical analogy where errors faults and failures are considered. The errors are something that cannot be seen, eg, a defect in the material. One has to prevent the errors becoming faults, therefore, a test process is required, say ultrasonic testing.

Then you have processes for trying to detect faults such as bolts becoming overstressed and again an inspection process would be in place. You need to make sure that the faults do not create a failure. If you do have a failure you need to have processes in that will mimise the effects of that failure. I find this a very reasonable way of looking at these matters.

I would like to support Professor Blockley's comments on vulnerability. In looking at the risk from bridge bashing one of the key issues is the vulnerability of the bridge. We need to be careful to look at the vulnerability of the bridge itself and not necessarily take account, in the first instance, of the control measure we put in to reduce the risk of an incident happening.

E Hambly

I recently watched a low bridge for a couple of hours last year. I was fascinated to see how container lorries approached it. The drivers didn't get out to check the relative heights. They drove slowly under the bridge listening whether they were scratching or not. The container lorries were so large that they would have simply lifted the bridge off if an impact had occurred.

Professor Blockley

Concerning probabilities and small projects, even with large projects the use of probabilistic risk assessment is at least misleading and at best downright dangerous. The numbers that result are, more or less, meaningless. I think this is dangerous in the wrong hands. The problem is one of interpretation. If you talk about 10^{-6} or the like, there is a statisitical connotation to that. We think of that as one in 10^6 is what it is intended to mean. In fact, the number is derived by a process that has little to do with statistical frequency. It is acceptable for us if we know what we are talking about but very dangerous if it is used by people outside of our particular discipline. I would therefore ask that we don't focus on probabilistic risk assessment but focus on hazard management.

With respect to small projects I didn't have time to elucidate some of the advice I might give to the question of how to deal with small projects. It is really about quality management, about what I call banana skin management, using the three Rs : Remove, Reduce, Remedy type thinking in order to deal with the hazards as you see them. I would like to make a further point concerning the relationship between safety and cost and profitability of organisations. There was study by the HSE a year or two ago called 'Costs of Accidents at Work'. This was an excellent study showing the relationship between cost and the number of accidents. The methodology was in my opinion a good methodology. The cost of accidents is very great and swamps other things. There is increasing evidence about the relationship between safety management, quality management, whatever term you adopt ,with respect to safety and profitability.

L. Howe, AEA Technology.

One would be forgiven, until a few minutes ago, for thinking that risk assessment was entirely about safety. We had a presentation earlier about the Channel Tunnel and it would have been fascinating to have an anlysis of the risks to escalating costs and the risks to late delivery.

N.Smith, Parkman.

In Professor Blockley's paper there are two statements concerning the construction industry. One states that the safety record is poor but the other statement : 'Until safety culture is improved the situation will just get worse', is alarming. I would like to ask how he arrived at this conclusion and what steps are necessary to put that culture right.

Professor Blockley

If you look at the statistics, there was some disagreement earlier about the relativity of it but three accidents a week or three deaths a week is pretty severe. The safety culture is a much more complex issue. It is really about good management, the culture of the organisation and as I see it the BPR movement, the Business Process Re-engineering movement is a way in which you can alter the culture of an organisation and it is up to senior management.

Professor Baker

I can't let Professor Blockley escape with having his earlier comments about safety and probability. I think the analogy would be in believing that the stresses that you calculate are stresses that you see in structures. Absolutely not, we don't normally measure stresses and we don't normally evaluate probabilities. I think there is much uncertainty in the calculation methods we use. Also probabilities are just tools to reach decisions, it is not the probability at the end of the day we use to gain information and we can't assess risk unless we can evaluate the hazard and look at the probability of something happening. They are both equally important.

SESSION 3
The beneficial application of risk assessment/management concepts

Methods That Apply to QRA in the Construction Industry

J Mather, C D Emery and P Fewtrell, W S Atkins Ltd

1 INTRODUCTION

This paper describes a feasibility study being undertaken for the Health and Safety Executive to develop a method for the collection of data to provide information on the criteria required to ensure the safe design of systems and products in civil, mechanical and structural engineering projects and to aid in the appraisal of risk assessments.

The work is part of a Call-off Contract between HSE and W S Atkins Ltd for Research in the fields of Safety and Risk across the whole range of activities undertaken by HSE.

The central theme to the project is the development of a semi-quantitative risk assessment methodology using a "Risk Matrix". It is intended that this system would provide managers, designers and inspectors of construction activities with a simple and inexpensive means of obtaining a measure of risk of projects and determining the acceptability of that value. It is envisaged that the matrix would contain the identified hazards for each type of operation undertaken during civil, mechanical and structural projects. The matrix would also need to contain historical data on accidents and some measure of the quality of management, supervision and other pertinent factors for the site in question in order to be able to perform and evaluation.

The acquisition of data is an essential element in this evaluation of the matrix. Most published data is insufficient in detail to use for this purpose. It is considered that a valuable source of data could be the reports prepared by the HSE Field Consultant Group (FCG) Officers as a part of their duties of inspection and control of construction sites. The format of current reports does not readily lend itself to the collection of such data.

The initial phase of the work is a feasibility study of the concept. This study has looked broadly at the issues involved in developing the Risk Matrix and at the acquisition of data. This has been done with reference to a limited number of construction activities ie Scaffolding, Cranage and Falsework. Future phases will go on to fully develop the matrix and to set up systems for data collection for continual refinement of the matrix.

The scope of work for the feasibility study is as follows:

* To develop a classification method which may be used in Field Consultant Group (FCG) reports to log the various technical factors which can then be used to create a risk-based matrix for civil, mechanical and structural engineering activities, initially using a limited range of topics.

* To develop a means of categorising the likely range of quality for each factor developed in the matrix.

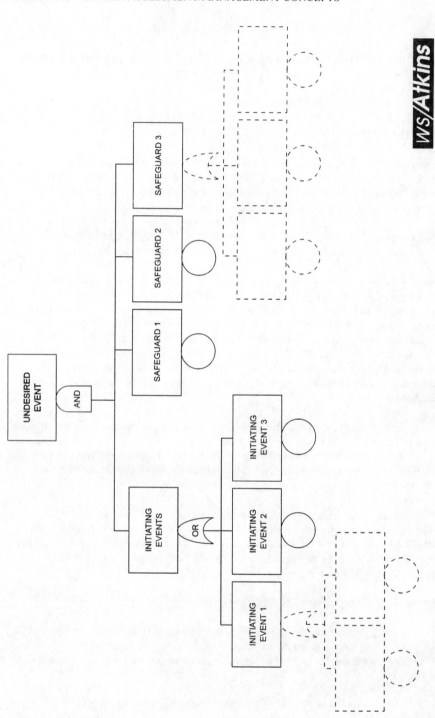

Fig. 1. Fault tree

♦ To develop suitable method(s) which could be used to apportion appropriate weighting factors within the risk matrix to assist in quantifying risk at the design stage of permanent and temporary structures and methods of work in civil, mechanical and structural projects.

2 QUANTIFIED RISK ASSESSMENT

Quantified Risk Assessment was developed in the Nuclear Industry to justify the design and operation of plant for which severe consequences could occur if containment measures for hazardous substances and ionising radiation fail. As methodologies have developed it has become widely used by designers, operators, planners and regulators to determine the acceptability of safety measures adopted for hazardous plant, equipment and industrial activities. These developments have also included extending QRA as a tool for financial decision making. In the UK safety legislation is moving away from prescriptive regulations and towards a risk based approach.

The basic and simple definition for Risk is normally depicted as an equation ie

RISK=PROBABILITY (or FREQUENCY) x CONSEQUENCE

Probability is determined as the number of times an undesirable event may occur in a given time period, normally reduced to events per year and Consequence is normally determined as deaths or injuries resulting from that event. This gives Risk in terms of deaths/injuries per year.

Other Consequences could be determined eg financial loss, environmental damage.

Quantified Risk Assessment is a 4 step process:

Step 1 Hazard Identification - HAZOP (Hazard and Operability) Studies, Check lists and FMECA (failure Modes, Effects and Criticality Analysis are formal methods. HAZOP has now been developed for a wide range of industries, engineering practices and activities.

Step 2 Determination of Consequences of each Credible, Identified, Undesirable Event - For process plant this could involve complex calculations of gas dispersion, fire and explosion events requiring data on population distributions and workforce movements. The complexity required will depend upon the substances involved and the level of accuracy required. For simple events such as inert dropped loads effects can be readily estimated.

Step 3 Determination of the Frequency of each Credible, Identified, Undesirable Event - Fault and Event Tree analysis are formal methods. These can become quite complex and in most cases frequencies determined are subject to significant uncertainties. Uncertainties are introduced in the data for failure rates of equipment, which may be taken out of context or statistically inaccurate and in determining probabilities of human actions. Figure 1 shows an outline Fault Tree. The undesired event occurs as a result of an initiating event (left hand side) at an estimated frequency together with the failure of safeguards (right hand side). The cause of the initiating events and safeguards are determined by expanding the tree to basic events for which data is available. The undesired event frequency (f_E) is therefore in the simplest case:

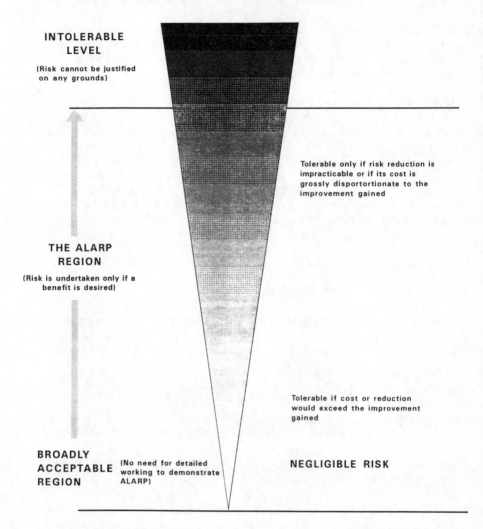

INTOLERABLE LEVEL

(Risk cannot be justified on any grounds)

Tolerable only if risk reduction is impracticable or if its cost is grossly disportortionate to the improvement gained

THE ALARP REGION

(Risk is undertaken only if a benefit is desired)

Tolerable if cost or reduction would exceed the improvement gained

BROADLY ACCEPTABLE REGION

(No need for detailed working to demonstrate ALARP)

NEGLIGIBLE RISK

Fig. 2. Levels of risk and ALARP

$$f_E = \Sigma_{ij} \ f_i \times p_j$$

where f_i = the frequency of the initiating event i

p_j = probability that safeguard j is failed

In practice it is likely that no all safeguards will protect against all initiating events combinations of safeguard failures may be required before the undesired event occurs. The structure of the tree will then be more complex. In evaluating the tree the individual initiating event and safeguard pairings will occur in the separate cut-sets which are added to give the overall frequency of the top event.

The Fault Tree approach is useful in comparing different designs or operating regimes and where a good estimate of Risk is required. Even in the best cases results should be regarded as accurate to only within 1 or 2 orders of magnitude. Fault trees analysis is a time consuming and therefore expensive process and is normally only used where risks are significant.

In cases where a rough estimate of risk only is required, historical data can be used. For simple activities, particularly those involving human actions this type of estimate is probably as accurate as any other, although any changes which have occurred since the data was collected should be allowed for.

Step 4 Comparison of Risk with Predetermined Criteria - Criteria for Risk have been developed by considering historical data such as the Fatality Accident Rate (FAR)[1]. For the construction industry the FAR is about 5×10^{-8} per hour. Taking a 2000 hour working year, the frequency of death for an individual worker is about 1×10^{-4} or about 1 in 10,000 year. The Health and Safety Executive have also developed criteria for major hazards installations[2]. The major underlying principle is ALARP (As Low As Reasonably Practicable). Figure 2 depicts the principle. If the risk of a death is less than about $1 \times 10_{-6}$ per year than no further action to reduce risk is required. If the risk is grater than $1 \times 10_{-3}$ per year it is unacceptable. In between is the ALARP region where further justification such as Cost Benefit Analysis or a revisiting of the risk calculations to determine accuracy and sensitivity is required.

3 THE RISK MATRIX

The Risk Matrix is an attempt to bring the principles of risk assessment into civil, mechanical and structural projects in a simplified but effective methodology.

Figure 3 shows the Risk Matrix. each element is an activity used in a major projects. The 3 activities chosen to test the matrix are:

1)   Scaffolding

ii)   Falsework

iii)   Cranage

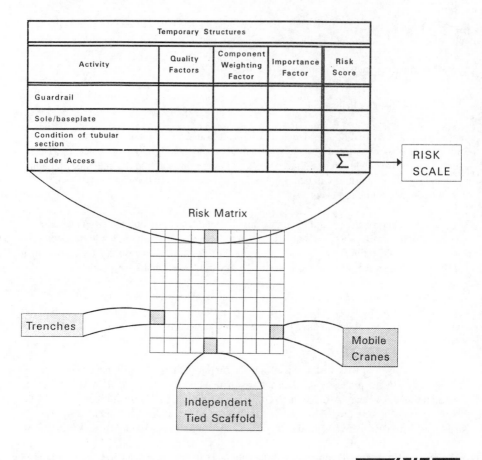

Fig. 3. Risk Matrix

A series of initiating events have been identified for each element which could cause either collapse of the structure of equipment, which in turn may bring about injuries to the workforce or the public, or a hazard to the workforce from tripping and falling type accidents. Generic events identified for the first of the trial elements ie scaffolding, is shown in Table 1.

In order to quantify the total risk for each element, from section 2 above, some measure of the frequency of the initiating events, the effectiveness of safeguards and the magnitude of the consequences need to be included, therefore 3 factors have been introduced to evaluate the matrix ie

(i) component weighting factor (fw) based upon the frequency of failure of the component or group of components from historical data.

(ii) quality factor (pq) based upon a considered opinion of the actual activity standard judged against codes of practice or guidance notes.

(iii) importance factor (ci) serving as a hazard/accident severity ranking.

The risk for each initiating event of group of initiating events can be evaluated as:

$$\text{Risk} = f_w \times p_q \times c_i$$

3.1 Component Weighting Factor

There is a small amount of published data on accidents in civil, mechanical and structural projects. The Health and Safety Executive itself has issued a number of reports[3-8]. However the detail is unsufficient to be able to determine precise initiating events.

For example, 1981-85 data[3] includes 739 deaths in total, for Scaffolding the following figures are given:

23 deaths were scaffolders.

24 deaths occurred during scaffold erection, of which 11 were due to inadequate edge protection, 5 were due to platforms slipping, 2 were due to scaffold collapse, 1 was due to no platform provided and for 5 no cause was specified.

18 deaths occurred due to falls from Tower Scaffolds, 12 during maintenance activities and 16 of these were said to be due to poor management/supervision.

49 deaths occurred due to falls from scaffolds and other working places. 19 of these were due to lack of guard rails and toe boards, 26 occurred during maintenance, 2 were due to scaffold collapse and 65% were due to unsafe systems of work/management.

12 deaths occurred during scaffold dismantling, 8 were due to lack of edge protection, 6 due to unsafe systems of work and 2 due to scaffold collapse.

TABLE 1

Identified Initiating Events for Scaffolding

1. DESIGN CONSIDERATIONS
Adequacy of:

- measures to provide stability and rigidity
- scaffold to carry loads to supporting structures
- assumptions of ground conditions and founding structures
- allowances made for superimposed loads
- selection of duty appropriate to use
- compliance with minimum width regulations
- provisions made for storage of materials
- provisions for lifting/lowering of materials and equipment
- materials, proprietary products and equipment proposed in the temporary works solution
- quantity of materials used
- provisions for safe access (gangways, ramps, ladders etc)
- measures allowed for protection against falling for people and materials (nets, fans, chutes) etc.
- measures to protect the general public
- guardrails/intermediate rails
- toeboards
- platform boards

2. MANAGEMENT

Adequacy of management with respect to:

- development of design brief
- development of working procedures for erection/in use/dismantling
- development of safety policy and procedures
- planning of the construction works
- provision of sufficient PPE
- provision of material resources
- training of workforce
- provision of trained workforce
- communications with sub-contractors, other contractors, visitors, adjacent enterprises, local authorities
- provision of site security

- site supervision of works
- site records (inspections)
- storage, maintenance and control of materials
- site housekeeping arrangements
- handover arrangements
- warning notices to workforce

- warning notices to general public
- special inspection records (eg adverse weather conditions)
- additional inspection records (equipment other than scaffolding material

3. MATERIALS/EQUIPMENT

Adequacy of:

- condition of materials/equipment in use
- storage arrangements
- standard of refurbishment
- maintenance
- quality control

4. WORKMANSHIP

Adequacy of:

- general compliance with design drawings/sketches
- founding/support conditions
- use of metal baseplates
- measures of sloping ground
- use of timber soleplates
- verticality of standards
- horizontal ledgers
- bracing
- transoms
- through ties
- reveal ties
- putlog blade supports
- staggered joints
- bay lengths
- couplers and fittings
- drilled-in fixings
- associated wire or band ties
- mixing of different materials/equipment (incompatibility)
- proprietary scaffolding
- platform boards (thickness/condition)
- space between boards
- minimum/maximum board overhand
- overlapping boards
- fixing of protective sheeting/netting etc
- fixing of access ladders (including projection above platform levels)

Conclusions that can be drawn are limited to: 113 of 739 (15.3%, 23 per year) of deaths were caused by Scaffolding faults, but there may be some double counting in the figures, and that 38 if 85 (44.7%) involved lack of toe boards or guard rails.

Therefore if 100 component weighting factor units are shared across the whole matrix, Scaffolding should have 15 component weighting factor units divided between the identified initiating events, of which toe board and guide rail failures would count as approximately 3.5 each.

Further data is being sought from company sources but it may be necessary to combine those identified initiating events which have common safeguards an similar consequences to fit the available data. Should suitable data not be available initially, expert opinion will be used to set the factors using a statistical method such as Pair Comparisons.

Future phases of the study will look in detail at a re-structuring of the format of the HSE Field Consultant Group (FCG) reports in order to collect data. The factors can be modified on a rolling basis as data from FCG reports and other sources becomes available.

3.2 Quality Factor

It is considered there are a number of elements to take account of in determining values for the safeguards against failures. It is suggested these are:

Design methods
Management
Materals/Equipment and,
Workmanship

These are a group of high level factors which each site activity can be assessed against. It would not be feasible to use a generic set of quality factors because for each activity it may be required to score a particular factor unique to that activity. Each quality factor needs to be broken down into constituent elements. A score can then be attached to each factor. It is important to ensure that all scores are normalised within the risk methodology.

The method of assessing will involve converting expert judgement into numerical form. A scoring system approach as used in safety auditing can be used. In this the inspector will complete a proforma checklist containing questions on the adequacy of each identified safeguard component with respect to each relevant high level factor with a 0-10 points score. An average can then be taken. It is considered that this approach will work most effectively for the assessor if one signifies totally inadequate/ineffective and 10 signifies best practice. This is the inverse of the requirement for risk quantification, where the lower the value, the best is the safeguard: therefore in the risk calculation these scores will be adjusted.

Table 1 shows a sample checklist for scaffolding.

3.3 Importance Factor
The importance factor is seen as being directly related to the activity. It would be a score that reflects the possible consequences should an accident occur. The scoring range could include factors such as:

number of on-site people likely to be affected
number of public likely to be affected
consequence of accident (fatality, major, minor)

The importance factor could be developed from past knowledge of similar accidents form source such as the HSE publications[3-8]. As for the component weighting factor, the importance factors could be reviewed on a rolling basis as data from FCG reports is collected.

Scoring could be as an estimate of the number of people likely to be killed or seriously injured by the event. It is likely for most initiating events this will be 1 person. However in events such as collapse of scaffolding, falsework or a crane in an area with public access there could be many more affected. Less serious injuries could be given a fractional value.

3.4 Risk Values

Risk values will be calculated by multiplying the component weighting factors, quality factors and importance factors for each component or group of components in the matrix. Adding the scores would determine risk for each activity The risk values computed will, of course, be relative not absolute. They will enable a comparison of activities at a site to determine where resources should be diverted to reduce risks.

Within the matrix itself there could be cross-linking between similar components of different activities so that there is consistency and no double counting.

It should also be possible to develop an ALARP system. High scores above a predetermined value would be unacceptable, low scores would be considered tolerable and further justification would be required be a range of scores between these two.

4 DISCUSSION

Quantified Risk Assessment (QRA) has provided the basis for decision making in land use planning and for site licensing of Major Hazards Industries including Nuclear, Chemical and Petrochemical for a number of years. More recently QRA has been included as a requirement in Formal Safety Assessments in the Offshore Oil & Gas Industry following recommendations by Lord Cullen after the Piper Alpha disaster[9]. Risk assessment has also a requirement in safety in the workplace as part of the 1992 Management of Health and Safety at Work Regulations, commonly known as the "pack of six" and the recent DCM Regulations. Health and Safety legislation in general is moving away from the prescriptive approach towards risk based approach.

The major advantage is not in the generation of numerical values of risk, because even in the best cases the value calculated is likely to be only accurate to 1 or 2 orders of magnitude, but in the logical and structured approach which causes those undertaking such exercises need to adopt.

The work undertaken to date has shown that QRA can also be applied to activities in the Construction Industry. A fully quantitative methodology for Risk Assessment would be extremely difficult and time consuming to apply in this field due to the nature of the activities which are manually orientated. Human factors analysis can sometimes be used in these circumstances however this is currently an inexact science even when studying well defined simple tasks. A much more appropriate methodology here is the semi-quantitative approach that is commonly used in safety auditing. This gives the major benefit that Risk Assessment provides ie a logical, structured approach to safety considerations. It also gives a numerical risk value, which can be compared directly with acceptability criterial figures, but based upon expert judgement rather than costly detailed analysis. Such systems can be more accurate than the detailed analysis in some circumstances.

The Risk Matrix methodology investigated in this work aims to combine the advantages of the semi-quantitative expert judgement approach with hard data from historical incidents to assist designers and site managers of civil, mechanical and structural projects to determine the relative importance of safety issues and to minimise risk. Much further work is needed to determine the full potential of the methodology but the early considerations are that it could prove an extremely useful tool.

The major problem in the development is the lack of suitable data to use in determining the component weighting and importance factors. Other sources are being sought such as information from companies operating in this field. If this proves unsuccessful, it may be necessary initially to use statistical methods to generate these factors using expert judgement.

It is intended that this study will go on to develop a format for HSE Inspectors to collect data in the future. Thus greater accuracy can be built into the factors as this becomes available.

5 CONCLUSIONS

1. The Risk Matrix system described in this paper has the potential to provide a useful, simple and effective semi-quantitative QRA methodology in civil, mechanical and structural projects.

2. Further work is required to develop the factors which determine the risk values for components, groups of components and activities.

3. Hazards for the three activities chosen to investigate the methodology ie Falsework, Scaffolding and Cranage, have been identified. These can form the basis for the collection of data by the HSE FCG Inspectors to provide a continual updating of matrix factors.

6 REFERENCES

1. Risk: Analysis, Perception, Management, Royal Society 1992

2. The Tolerability of Risk from Nuclear Power Stations, Health and Safety Executive, HMSO 1992

3. Blacksport Construction: A Study of Five Years Fatal Accident in the Building and Civil Engineering Industries, Health and Safety Executive, HMSO 6/88

4. Construction Health and Safety 1977-8, Health and Safety Executive, HMSO

5. Construction Health and Safety 1979-80, Health and Safety Executive, HMSO

6. Construction Health and Safety, 1981-2, Health and Safety Executive, HMSO

7. Fatal Accidents Construction 1977, Health and Safety Executive, HMSO

8. Health and Safety Statistics 1979-80, Health and Safety Executive, HMSO

9. The Public Enquiry into the Piper Alpha Disaster, The Hon Lord Cullen, HMSO

Factors Affecting Safety, Cost and Quality of Scaffolding

M JAMES   Health & Safety Executive

INTRODUCTION

This paper is concemed with the variety of the risks which threaten the success of any project. It looks at how these might be best dealt with, and suggests this is best done at the design stage. It also considers the possibility of developing a simple design method which will encourage the consideration of all forms of risk in an integrated manner in a pro-active design process.

The paper uses scaffolding as an example to illustrate how any type of project might generally benefit from the use of such a design process when applied by an experienced designer, and to help identify some of the possible design difficulties. Scaffolding is considered to be appropriate for this purpose because:-

1)   it is a relatively simple type of equipment, both in construction and organisation making it possible to give clear examples.

2)   it has been in use for a long time, more or less in its present form. Therefore a considerable amount of information and experience has accumulated which, although still far from being comprehensive, can be used to illustrate the relationship between the risks as might affect various aspects of this type of equipment such as safety, cost and quality.

3)   these structures are nonnally of such small scale and relative low cost that if the proposed design methods were relevant to them they would almost certainly be relevant to more complicated and costly projects.

Some considerations are also given to the benefits of specifying the acceptable level of risk at the start of any project, how these might be identified, understand and used in a design process.

GENERAL

The basic assumptions made in this paper are that:-

1) all products or projects are made or carried out for a reason, therefore they have a FUNCTION, PURPOSE or DUTY.

2)   the designer or client etc. set out to make the project a SUCCESS in meeting this function, purpose or duty in whatever way that might be envisaged.

The discussions that follow are all concemed with these fairly uncontroversial propositions.

To complete any product or project will, in most cases, require the carrying out of a quite complicated set of operations. These operations, perhaps rightly, often receive far more attention than the main purpose of the project. For example there could be more concern over, or concentration on, obtaining the right materials, building to programme or organising the required transport, than worrying about the overall purpose of the project. Where this occurs, there is often a danger the real reason for the project may be so ignored or subordinated to the means of producing it, that the project may no longer adequately meet its intended purpose or serve the original function.

This failing could be avoided if the function was always properly and clearly defined and reiterated at each stage of the project in a manner which would help direct and control the activities used to create the project or product.

The first step in being able to do this would be adequately and suitably define the function that it would be uncontroversial and could be clearly understood. At present this would probably mean using a descriptive vocabulary which could then present difficulties because there might be many ways of describing the project. In the case of scaffolding, for example, there are many different definitions of a scaffold, such as that in the British Standard Code of Practice 5973, the Construction Regulations or in dictionaries (for examples see those in appendix E). These have varying degrees of practicality and clarity so as to cause possible confusion as to the main objective of scaffolds. If descriptive terms are to be used they ought to be clear about the purpose of the project. As an example the following definition is proposed for scaffolding in this paper which can be contrasted with those in appendix E and, it is suggested, would be more useful in directing attention to its purpose.

'A temporary structure used to support a temporary working platform, the working platform itself and any attached temporary means of gaining access to that platform'

This definition clearly gives attention to the central and only purpose of the scaffold, to carry a working platform, and on its nature i.e., that it is temporary. It stresses that the work platform is the most important part of the scaffold, with the supporting structure and the means of access as subsidiary functions of allowing the work platform to perform as intended.

However it may still be inadequate, no matter how accurate it is particularly for numerical design processes. Therefore it will help if the function of a project can be examined and described in more detail in judging how the purpose of a project is assessed.

To be able to judge how a project meets its function the CRITERIA for the products functional performance must be understood and defined. These criteria, or AIM's, can be grouped under one of a series of concerns such as safety, efficiency and effectiveness. Therefore, in effect the SUCCESS of a project can be assessed by the degree that these AIM's are met. It will fail to the extent which any of the AIM's are not achieved, for instance to the degree a working platform provides a safe, economic and efficient place of work.. It then follows that the dangers, or risks, which might prevent the AIM's from being realised, must be controlled if a **failure** is to be avoided. It might then be possible to so define the risks to the AIM's that they become controlling parameters for the design. it is clear that to be able to do this effectively will require that ALL the relevant criteria are taken into account in the design process.

113

The logic of the above is reinforced when considering how the carrying out of any design using only a limited set of requirements cannot ensure a project will have the most effective or successful outcome. Success can only be arrived at if all the AIM's are fully appreciated and the risks to them properly evaluated within a 'sensible' balance between the conflicts raised by different AIM's.

The common situation where inadequate concentration has been given to a projects function (such as house or factory), as already mentioned, is then frequently further compounded by failing to consider all the criteria for the performance of that function. While generally most products or projects are expected to achieve some success in reaching some expectation, or even to meet a specification for quality and cost, in common practice these performance requirements normally represent only a partial set of AIM's and considering only these partially, is too erratic a method to ensure that any project will be a success. Many projects will therefore fail without anyone really recognising this, but still with serious consequences for the client and society in general.

There is clearly a need to develop a design philosophy that can help the designer give proper consideration to these matters and if the process of complying with the AIM's is to be part of a logical design method, it also follows that to guarantee a reliable level of success, the process will have to be part of a deliberate action. Therefore it can be argued that a successful project is one that conforms to those AIM's which have been deliberately chosen, rather than any that might have been arrived at through some lucky accident or other set of happy coincidences.

A definition of success can be stated as being:-

'Achieving the performance levels which were either deliberately <u>chosen</u> or <u>inferred</u> when a project was first considered, or as may have been amended as the project developed.

As a project is designed to succeed, the above definition should then be built into the definition of its function. In the example of a scaffold, the definition already given could include such things as bosun's chairs, ladders, and trestles in addition to those structures we might normally consider as scaffolds. It would apply to any means that could be a way of providing any temporary work place. However there will be many safety, cost and quality requirements for such structures (eg. for scaffolding there will be safety considerations such as the dangers of falls; cost considerations perhaps over the probability of low productivity; and quality issues concerning the ability to do a reasonable job), that might limit the types of equipment really suitable for a particular application. Therefore a rider could be added to the definition of a scaffold to include the criteria by which its success can be judged. This might be:-

The platform to be of such a nature and at such a suitable position, that work can be done from it on some other structure in a safe, efficient and effective manner.'

The amended definition now recognises that all the dangers or risks which could adversely influence the achievement of those AIM's of a project already described have been properly considered and the means of dealing with them have been built into the design.

However to be able to claim that the project is a success, will still require the designer to have agreed the limits to the risks to the AIM's and in some measurable form so they may be checked and confirmed.

For example if we wished to know if a piece of plant was successful from a safety point of view, we would need to have had some idea of what level of safety was intended in the first place. In the same way some form of intended value for the quality and cost AIM's of the project would also need to be envisaged.

It may not mean that working to a set of AIM's will always result in the enhancement of a projects performance. For example, it would generally accepted that a project which is expensive (i.e. runs over budget), suffers accidents or is of a poor quality and cannot perform as intended, is a failure, although if such a performance was intended then, by the definition already stated, it could be regarded as a success.

Equally a project that produces unlooked for profits and performs as a Rolls-Royce when all the client looked for was a basic Mini, could also be a failure. Although, in most of such cases, any enhancements from the original specification would be accepted gratefully by the client, they could indicate the designer has committed too many resources to the project, or to certain aspects of the project which could cause detrimental effects elsewhere. It has therefore missed its AIM's.

The benefits of designing by defining the acceptable risks to the AIM's could well ensure that these risks are suitably controlled from the earliest stages of the project. The HSE has long been aware that the causes of most accidents have their origins in the early stages of the planning and design processes. Further the European Commission has also identified that it is far more cost effective to deal with risks in the early planning stages, as illustrated in the graph from their report, shown in fig 1.

Because we live in a far from ideal world to simply set out the AIM's of a project and assume these are achievable may not be so useful. With every activity there is always some degree of risk and the most useful guiding criteria for any design process could be the acceptable level of risk. Therefore establishing these acceptable levels of risk at the start of the planning/design process and using these to guide and control the development of the project will ensure that the risks will then be controlled in a logical manner and that the project will be more likely to be a success.

To summarise, the SUCCESS of any project is a measure of how its AIM's had been achieved after the risks to these AIM's have been first properly defined, measured and agreed as being essential to its PURPOSE or FUNCTION and then achieved within defined acceptable limits. In addition these AIM's must also have been achieved in some balanced manner as far as was reasonably possible.

THE AIMS OF A PROJECT

Before trying to propose an acceptable level of risk for any of the **AIM'S,** it is first necessary to decide what these AIM's should be. While the idea of quantifying the AIM's might be difficult because currently most AIM's are specified in a subjective manner, it is proposed that it might not be quite the same problem to specify the limit to the risk to AIM's or the limit to the level of risk the AIM's should be proof against.

There are complications to this simple statement because most plant or products must meet at least two sets of AIM'S. Basically these are those of the provider and those of the recipient i.e., of the contractor or manufacturer and those of the client. In addition within each of these sets there could be quite wide variations, such as where the customer is really many different users each with their own different sets of requirements.

For scaffolding, the AIM's will vary considerably from job to job but typically the clients could include the following:-

Safety AIM'S.
> # providing a reasonable degree of safety to the users
> and others in the area.

Cost AIM'S.
> # low cost.

Quality AIM'S.
> # providing a good work station.
> # having adequate strength,
> # giving minimum interference to other activities or causing minimal
> damage to the supporting structure.

The scaffolders aims on the other hand might include:-

Safety AIM'S.
> # capability of being erected, used and dismantled
> safely.

Cost AIM'S.
> #   giving a reasonable financial return.
> #   having low maintenance costs over a long life.
> #   having a minimum number of components and particularly having few types of
> components,
> #   being easily erected with a minimum number in the erection team giving a
> quick turnaround.

Quality AIM'S.
> #   being capable of meeting the demands of the clients.
> #   having great versatility.
> #   having adequate strength.

Lists such as these show that the AIM's of the various parties involved in a project may not be the same and it is therefore easy for conflicts and disputes to arise. The lists also highlight difficulties any one party might have in reconciling all of their own AIM's.

It is almost certain therefore, that with any project, certain compromises will have to be agreed between the various AIM's and most AIM's will be achievable only as far as is reasonably possible probably within a performance range. The designers problem is to find a suitably balanced arrangement where all the AIM's are in some form of reasonable relationship so that one set of AIM's, e.g. safety, will not fall too low in satisfying the AIM's in another area, such as cost or performance.

In the example of scaffolding, a low or negligible cost to the client must be balanced against giving a reasonable return to the scaffolder. Another example might be where the clients requirement for the provision of a good work station conflicts with the scaffolders requirements of limiting the number of components supplied.

The balancing of the relationship between the various AIM's and of their various values could be envisaged as describing a profile for the project. In the diagrammatic representation below it is imagined that a specific value can be awarded to the limitation to the risks to the various AIM's of a project. The line linking these would then be the project profile. Such a diagram illustrates that if the limits to one of the AIM's was amended, say to the profit margin, then all the values of the others would also have to be altered to some degree so giving a revised project profile.

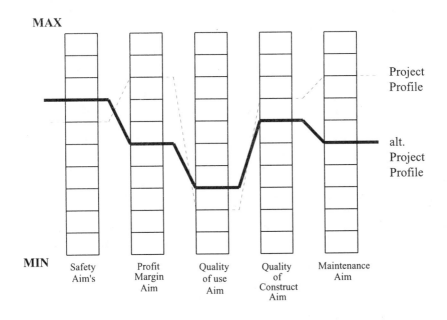

As already stressed the AIM's will have to be defined in some logical manner that will allow their values to be easily understood, perhaps in some form of range or band rating between a maximum and a minimum value, so they can be compared with each other. Certainly the common present methods of specifying most AIM's in some form of qualitative manner will not be suitable (except those for profit and costs), and it is possible that even the present way of looking at profits and costs will not be suitable as this does not deal with the limitation of the level of risk or measure its impact on the 'success' in the areas of the other AIM'S.

As it is so difficult to specify the acceptable limits to the risks to the AIM's for something as simple as scaffolding by common methods of analysis and interpretation it can be appreciated how much more so it will be for more complicated structures or equipment.

THE DATA CONCERNING RISKS

As already noted if the project is to be a success, the design must try to protect the AIM's from risk. The risks, their seriousness and their likelihood, need to be properly evaluated and understood if they are to be used in any design process.

Understanding and quantifying the allowable limits to the risks will need to be in a different manner than that used to describe risk itself if it is to be used in a specification. For instance, a specification for safety levels of $10(-4)$ could lead to arguments about whether the project complied with the specification if an accident occurs when the man hour total was only $10(-3)$ or did not occur until $10(-6)$. Such an argument would be pointless because the accident could by itself neither prove or disprove the safety level. The one exception perhaps being a specification for zero costs, zero accidents, etc. While such a specification is impossible to meet, at least it is quite clear.

A basic requirement in specifying allowable levels of risk is to have access to sufficient DATA of a suitable quality and relevance that the specification would be related to real situations, eg. data concerning the likely level of performance by the anticipated work force. Having such data would mean that the risks could be better understood, and therefore controlled, and the outcome of the design more accurately predicted.

As a first step in creating this data it would be necessary to determine where the risks came from and, perhaps, whose responsibility they were. There is also the question of how the data should be logged? Should it, for instance, be logged against management activities, the type of structure, the type of job, the environmental effects or on a time basis? (or should the risks be itemised in a general or more detailed manner?).

Logging all risks as being essentially a management problem, while undoubted true, may be such a very general approach that it might not succeed in identifying the roots of the problem and where the controls can be best applied.

It will certainly be necessary, at least initially, to look separately at the risks to the various AIM'S. The following brief review concerning the information on the risks to the safety, quality and cost AIM's applicable to scaffolding, is an example of how data may be accumulated, interpreted and used.

The safety risks It is possible to class these in either a general or detailed manner such as those that are applicable to all types of project and those that are specific to one aspect of one particular project. For instance those associated with scaffolds in general can be shown to be of concern to both client and scaffold contractor as is indicated in the following table which shows how hazardous the construction industry is and how hazardous scaffolding is within that industry.

Incident rates for fatal accidents.

All industries	**approx 2.0**
Construction industry only	**approx 10.0**
Scaffolding	**approx 15.0**

Notes.

1)   These are for 1,000,000 man days per annum.
2)   The figures in this table for all industries and for the construction industry are based on the HSC's 1992/3 report. The figure for scaffolding is partly based on various assumptions that attempt to define the man hours worked on scaffolds.

Another set of general figures for scaffolding accidents can be derived by comparing these with the percentage of accidents in the construction industry as a whole. Such a comparison shows that while up to 23% of all construction accidents could involve work on scaffolds, scaffolding itself represents only approx. 1.5% of the total value of the construction industry, gives further evidence that scaffolding is an hazardous occupation within a hazardous industry.

It is also possible to show the pattern of accidents in a more detailed manner as indicated in Appendix A. and Appendix B. It should be noted that while the type of information given in these Appendices allows the safety of various activities or situations to be assessed, this may still not give a sufficiently detailed analysis of the risk pattern for the purposes of a designer. The danger in trying to evaluate risks using too general information, while having some value, means that unnecessary resources could be committed to areas that do not need them while not properly covering those that are really vulnerable. This could also be quite detrimental by inhibiting potential areas of good performance by, what is in effect, a blanket approach.

The quality risks. For the client the risks of poor performance should be the most important consideration, for such risks most obviously affect the reason why the project is being carried out. However while they may be readily understood in a qualitative manner, they are much more difficult to quantify.

For instance, there is little or no data concerning quality risks with scaffolding and as the layout of a scaffold changes so much from job to job it makes it that much more difficult to collect meaningful data or to assess any that might be available. This problem is further compounded through it being normal for the use and layout of a scaffold to change as the work progresses, altering both the quality risks and the means of assessing them.

As a result many quality risks are both ignored and accepted. A scaffold having a wrong layout, being in the wrong place or being so unsafe that delays are caused to the client is often accepted as one of those things and all that is done is to take a mental note to avoid using that scaffold contractor again. No records are made to help in assessing this vital function, such as whether a particular type of working platform is suitable for its purpose to be a good work station.

Yet the ergonomic factors associated with the position, layout and nature of the work platform are bound to affect the work being done from it: such as by slowing down the productivity rate or on the quality of the work being achieved, which could have a major bearing on whether the resultant building meets the clients requirements.

For example, a person can best perform work when that work is in a convenient relationship to the persons body. How this is defined depends on both the size of the person and the job being done. For manipulative tasks the best position is to have a working level at between 50-100mm below the elbow, while for more delicate tasks the ideal is 50-100mm above the elbow. Most work done from scaffolds are at levels very different from these ideals and this must result in some reduction in the quality of the output in some places.

Where a person is expected to work long hours in a position that is not ideal, this will result in some reduction in the quality of the output and even increase the risk of injuries through backstrain etc. Therefore there will be many potential hidden risks arising out of the nature and position of the working platform that ultimately must reflect on the performance or quality of the final structure or product. These will perhaps add up to something far more significant than problems merely concerning the strength or layout of the scaffold.

For the scaffolding contractor the question of the ergonomic layout of a scaffold is strongly related to its versatility, whether it is possible to build it in the most suitable proximity to the work. The quality risks will also revolve around the level of maintenance required by the scaffold equipment (will it suffer a lot of handling damage for instance), and the amount of equipment, particularly different types of equipment, required on each job.

To summarise, even though the quality AIM's are probably the most important criterion in deciding whether a project is a success or not, for most cases at present it is only possible to describe such AIM's in a very general manner and there are few means of systematically recording any results or observations on the matter.

The financial risks. The cost risks are probably the most analysed item on any project, being generally appreciated or understood to a far greater extent than any of the others. However this appreciation is probably more concerned with the sums paid out rather than in understanding the risks to these costs or their significance.

Returning to the example of scaffolding, the overall average ratio of the value of the scaffolding sector in the construction industry to the total value of the industry is 1.5% referred to previously, suggests that scaffolds are of a relative minor financial concern. However, this hides the fact that this ratio is far higher and therefore far more important when the actual job being done from them is considered.

An indication of the real percentage of the cost of a scaffold in relation to the overall cost of the job they are required for, is given below. It is based on typical hire charges for fairly robust scaffolds.

the job	scaffold cost as a % of the total cost
CASE A Removing light buld from 6M high ceiling	75%
CASE B Redecorating/repointing a line of 1st and 2nd floor windows	33%
CASE C Repair of eaves to a 30M long by 4M high building.	25%
CASE D Construction of a 2 storey building.	20%

The above table indicates, that where the amount of the work increases, the ratio of the cost of the scaffolding to the total cost of the job falls. But it is also clear that the job would have to be really large to reduce the percentage to anywhere near the overall industry norm of 1.5%.

These costs could be easily put at risk by any delay in carrying out the work from the scaffold. If, for instance, the work was delayed by one week the % cost for case B would increase to around 40%, for case C to 28% and for case D to 22%. From the clients point of view scaffold costs usually represent 'dead' money, there are few apparent tangible lasting benefits from building the scaffold structure and they therefore represent major deviations from the cost AIM's.

As far as the scaffolder is concerned failure to get all the right scaffold materials to site at the right time or of having to go back to amend the layout of the scaffold because it had been incorrectly positioned, could seriously risk the profitability of the job. The nominal profit margins to the scaffolder, that is the money to him after only his immediate costs have been met, is quite limited and would almost certainly in the cases listed in the table, be wiped out if a two man team had to return to site for even the most minimal activity once the scaffold had been completed.

Again to summarise. The risks to the cost AIM's of a project should be seen both as those that affect it overall as well as those that relate to individual components of the project as the impact of the realisation of risk to quite minor components could easily undermine the cost AIM's for the whole project.

THE RELATIONSHIP BETWEEN THE VARIOUS AIM'S

If risks are to be properly tackled and designers encouraged to devote additional time to their control or elimination, then all the AIM's must be dealt with at the same time. To tackle any one aspect, i.e. the safety problem, without tackling the others will be both wasteful in resources and fail to achieve an optimum value for all aspects of the project. In addition failure to tackle all the risks at the same time may even undermine any limited controls put in place through a process of risk transfer i.e., by transferring the safety risks to the cost risks, the cost risks to the quality risks or the quality risks to the safety risks etc.

To be able to design the project properly, dealing with all the risks at the same time requires them to be linked together in some logical manner. This would be fairly logical because all types of risk are related to each although this relationship may be a little difficult to prove. It can be demonstrated in general by considering that every safety consideration has a cost issue which could be a typical 'add-on' cost of say providing and fitting sufficient accident prevention materials or the possible cost savings through preventing accidents. The HSE has produced a booklet entitled'The Cost of Accidents at Work'which shows a very clear link between profitability and safety showing the real magnitude of accident costs. It indicates that virtually every cost issue in effect also carries a safety one and vice versa.

Similarly, it can be argued that the risks to quality are also closely linked to those of cost and therefore of safety.

For example the following table indicates the link between safety cost and quality over a limited range of requirements for scaffolding. It suggests how these various risks are linked.

COST AND QUALITY RISKS

Typical risks Quality	Typical risks to Cost	Typical risks to Safety	General Reasons for these risks
Does not suit the job.	need to adopt lower quality or inefficiency	muscular/skeletal injuries, fall and falling objects	platform wrong height or width or inappropriate materials.
Requires frequent attention.	damage to scaffold or building, cost of accidents.	collapse, partial or total.	structurally unsound.
Blocks progress.	low productivity.	encourages short cuts.	time consuming to handle.
Permits accidents.	remedial costs.	permits accidents.	insufficient protection,

To summarise, risks are related to each other and to tackle them piecemeal is very inefficient and can possibly result in merely transferring the risk to other AIM'S. Therefore the most economic and efficient way of dealing with risk is in an integrated manner.

ACCEPTABLE LEVELS OF RISK

Any process that sets out to use the risks to the AIM's to control the design process will obviously have to tackle the problem of what is an acceptable level of risk and how this is to be envisaged. Examples have been given earlier on the possible difficulties of setting safety AIM's and it can be imagined that any limits to safety levels could become quite emotive. This would be true of other AIM's especially in circumstances concerning say environmental issues. Yet it is clearly unreasonable to expect any project to be totally free of risk and as with health and safety issues, any risk can only to be dealt with'so far as is reasonably practical'. This means, according to a legal judgement, that it is assumed the risk and the cost of avoiding it have been put on some set of scales in arriving at just what is a reasonably balanced solution. However it is obvious that many of the conclusions drawn in this manner would always be open to argument and is therefore of limited value to the designer.

A more useful approach might be in looking at those features that control risk, such as the quality of supervision, the aptitude of those doing the work, the level of training (especially the degree of refresher training), and the thoroughness of the planning and design.

There is no question that the factors that influence risk and the attitudes to acceptable risk, are very numerous and their inter-reaction multiplies the resulting options considerably, especially when the whole life variables are also added into the equation. It is probably true, however, that there is no need to examine every detail of a project in trying to set acceptable levels of risk. It may be possible to limit such an investigation to identifying the weakest links in the operational chain and consider whether these will be strong enough not to fail at an unacceptably low level. Following such a procedure could enable the strongest links to be similarly examined to check that an unnecessary amount of resources were not being wasted.

POSSIBLE ALTERNATIVE DESIGN METHOD

As already discussed the designers fundament task is to ensure the project is a success and that the risks to the AIM's are identified and controlled, that hazards are minimised and opportunities are maximised. The possible opportunities for improved efficiency, safety and effectiveness have not been discussed in this paper but could come from the more rapid identification of the likely problems at an early stage. This would then allow them to be dealt with at a lower cost; with a more effective use of materials, members and systems; and with the quicker, cheaper and more reliable provision of safety.

Yet despite the possibility of obtaining significant benefits, it is probable there would be a general resistance or reluctance to spending increased resources on achieving them. A typical example of this is perhaps again in the scaffolding industry where the statistics suggest a willingness to accept the risks that appear inevitable with its use in return for minimising the design and management control effort. This suggests there is little hope of traditional ways of design and management doing anything more than producing nominal progress.

However it can well be imagined that any design process trying to deal with the problems created by the multiplicity of the AIM's could easily require a large increase in the designers time. Yet it is clearly not reasonable to expect the designer to spend endless time in trying to rationalise the conflicts and restrictions in using qualitative values for the AIM's for some hard to understand benefit. Therefore any alternative design method would have to be so clearly beneficial to overcome this natural unwillingness on the part of many to adopt something new. If the AIM's are then to be used in a design process, a different approach will have to be developed which, in particular, recognises the need to limit any additional efforts on the part of the designer.

There could be three alternative ways of developing such an approach, all of which focus attention to some degree or other, on some or all of the performance or function requirements of a project.

A)   The first one is an all over 'add-on' approach and is by identifying and systematically eliminating the risks by working from lists of hazards based on experience and site records.

The idea behind this would be for the designer or planner to build in sufficient protection so as to minimise the hazards. (e.g. for scaffolding by cladding it with netting to prevent falling persons or falling materials).

This concept is further illustrated in appendix B.

The drawback with this approach is that it would encourage the piecemeal protection against risk and of the 'add-on' mentality, particularly as regards the provision of safety and is not likely to result in a major shift in the usual design approaches.

B)   A second method would be in the form of a revised 'add-on' approach which would attempt to place the added-on resources more accurately at the point where they are needed. This method would be in addition to considering the hazards and would quantify the variable standards of construction often found in many projects and then attribute a suitable partial safety factor to these relative to the expected work quality performance. In other words designing the product specifically for its likely use or mis-use, so that it is not only fit for its function but is also fit for the type of persons who will erect and use it. Appendix C illustrates this method for a scaffolding project.

The basic concept of this approach assumes that the performance of the more critical elements of the project could be measured over a series of jobs and the results banded according to whether they represented good, reasonable, or indifferent practice. For instance, a scaffold could be designed to correspond to the likely quality of workmanship or the likely degree of mis-use.

The benefits that could be obtained can be indicated by scaffolds where many of these, if built carefully to the Code of Practice, would have an overall factors of safety of around 10/12. The level of mis-use of scaffold structures is clearly indicated by the fact that despite this very high factor of safety there is still so much trouble with these structures. If the safety enhancement could be placed only where it was needed then there could be scope for not only reducing the accident rates but also reducing the amount of materials required in the scaffold, and therefore its costs, and perhaps enhancing the scaffolds performance.

It is interesting to note that some of the scaffold manufacturers are beginning to make greater use of prefabricated scaffolding components, allowing a reduction in the Factor of Safety at certain places so as to be more in line with normal engineering practice. However, prefabrication will also affect the versatility of the scaffold. This is one of the many trade-off problems when considering the different AIM'S.

C)   The third method of creating a suitable design philosophy could be to identify the essential elements within the project and then ensure that each is sufficient to cover the risks to the job. In the example of scaffolding, this would probably require a detailed analysis of the structure so that each element within it can be designed to comply with the overall AIM'S. Thus each element would become sufficient for its purpose but no more.

The criteria that govern a scaffolds success can be listed under a series of headings such as those following:-

   the scaffold structure itself,
   the environment where it is to be built,
   the management control (including the structural design) and the variations in the
   structure in various time periods.

These elements could then be examined in greater detail by being further subdivided allowing the risks and requirements for each of these smaller elements being evaluated. This process could continue looking at smaller and smaller elements so that the smallest component from which the most important risk problems grow, can be identified. a possible process is illustrated in appendix D.

Examining the risks to a project in some form of systematic manner could have two major benefits:-

1)   Firstly it would ensure that all aspects of a project, all its AIM'S, complied in some way with the function of the project and therefore could be included in a general form of accounting. There is little doubt that within our present society where a item is not measurable then it is usually so relegated to be ignored. Therefore the suggested process would help to ensure all aspects of a project complied with their AIM'S.

2)   Secondly it should help to highlight areas that are inefficient and prone to risk. This will mean that the designer can concentrate efforts at those places giving the best return for the design effort. This could also help to get the most out of the design effort by encouraging the innovation of new ideas through pinpointing the weakness', achieving an essential benefit of making the additional effort with such a design process that much more acceptable.

CONCLUSIONS

It seems probable that a considerable amount of resources, human and financial, are being lost because many aspects implicit within a design are ignored or dealt with in an unstructured manner. With the example of scaffolding it seems clear that there is plenty of evidence to show there is plenty of room to achieve better results. It could well be assumed that a 5% improvement in the control of risks could result in an annual financial benefit of approx. £30m, a safety benefit in reducing fatalities by 2-3 and major accidents by around 25 and give some difficult to quantify improvements in the quality of the work performed from them. It is also probable that similar improvements could be obtained in costs and quality.

The ability of the designer to design out risks will , however, always be subjected to what can be achieved on site. No matter how well any structure, product or system is designed and planned, it will still perform badly if it is not used and managed properly. The accident statistics on scaffolds indicate that more than 67% of the accidents happen to the user. This suggests the site control of these structures is poor. This then also suggests that the site control over costs and quality could also be poor. In this paper it is suggested that such poor quality of site management could be allowed for in the design of the project, if this is different from that assumed then there will be little chance of the project becoming a success and this failure could reflect unfairly on the designer. By specifying the value of the risks to the AIM's, or perhaps specifying the acceptable levels of risk in a form that could be agreed by all those involved, including the client, the responsibilities on the designer might be limited to a reasonable level.

ACKNOWLEDGEMENTS.

Grateful thanks are given to Mr.A.Maitra for permission to quote from his research and to Mr.J.Comish of SGB Youngmans for help in producing the table on scaffolding costs.

REFERENCES

British Standard Code of Practice BS5973 1993 Access and Working scaffolds and special scaffold structures in steel.
Ergonomics, standards and guidelines for designers. BSI ISBN 0 580 15391 6
Cost of Accidents at Work. Health and Safety Series booklet HS(G)96
Successful Health and Safety Management. Health and Safety Series booklet HS(G)65
Construction (Working Places) Regulations
Health and Safety Commission Annual Report 1992/3 HSE Books
Annual abstract of Statistics 1994 Central Statistical Office HMSO ISBN 0 11 620605 5
Social Security Statistics 1994 HMSO ISBN 0 11 762226 5
Safety and Health in the Construction Sector. Commission of the European Communities.
ISBN 92-826-6037-0

APPENDIX A.

1.   # the cause of the failure.

not properly built	31%
overturned	13%
failure of boards	4%
overload of ties	4%
failures of components	4%
eg braces transoms, standards etc	

2.   # the sequence of the work in time.

scaffold type	during erection	use	dismantling
tube & fitting	22%	60%	18%
system scaffold	10%	67%	23%
tower scaffold	6%	83%	8%

3.   # the type of scaffold used.

comparison between the accidents on a type of scaffold and that scaffolds share of the market.

scaffold type	% accidents	% markets
tube & fitting	33	33
system scaffolds	9	15
tower scaffold	34	12

4.   # the trades who suffer accidents

	Type of Accident			
	Falls		struck by	
	Fatal	Non-fatal	Fatal	Non-fatal
bricklayers	118	5	12	0
scaffolders	118	18	19	0
concreters	39	0	11	0
demolition workers	12	2	0	0
labourers	185	12	48	0
steelfixers	2	0	1	0
maintenance workers	52	4	5	0
steel erectors	21	0	2	0

5.   # the nature of the accident.

Type of incident	number of accidents
falls from scaffolds	504
collapse of scaffold	210
struck by falling objects off scaffolds	136
slips, trips and falls on scaffolds	29
electrocutions during use or erection of scaffolds	32

6.   # how the size of company influences the incident rates.

see fig 1.

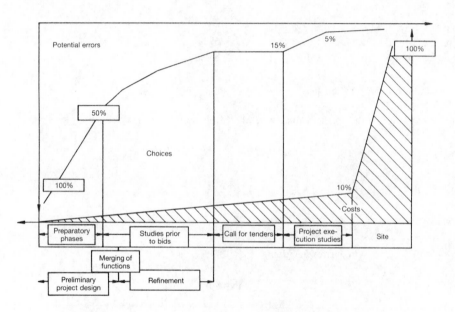

Figure 1

APPENDIX B.

This table suggests how numerical values could be given to the frequency and consequence components of risk for scaffolding operations.

HAZARD	TRIGGER	FREQUENCY (Scale 1-3)	CONSEQUENCE (Scale 1-4)
Fall from height	Inadequate guarding	3	1-4
Slips & trips	Poor surface Surface obstructions	1	1-3
Falling objects	Inadequate guards	3	1-4
Collapse/failure (partial/total)	Overload Inadequate ties Poor maintenance Poor quality	1	1-4
Striking against	Projecting items	3	1-3
Contact with moving parts incl transport	Layout	1	1-4
Electrocution	Layout	1	2-4
Exposure to weather	Inadequate protection	1	1-2
Chemical & similar hazards	Inadequate protection Poor control	1	1-3
Lifting/strain injury	Poor layout	3	1-3
Flying objects	Inadequate protection	2	1-2

COST/QUALITY FACTORS

Unsuitable for the job ie wrong height, too weak, insufficient space	Poor planning Inadequate specification	2	2-4
Insufficient materials	Poor planning	2	1-3
Need for frequent changes	Unsuitable for the job, poor planning and control	1	1-4
Loss and damage to materials	Poor control	3	1-3
Slow to erect and modify	Unsuitable for the job	2	2-3

APPENDIX C.

This table suggests some of the areas where the use of appropriate partial safety factors could enhance the safety of the total scaffold without requiring the scaffold in general to be designed to the same level.

Gamma Factors Situation	Scale Band (scale 1-10)	Relative Importance (rating 1-4)
Footing/Foundation	3-9	3
Standards	5-9	2
Ledgers/Braces	6-8	3
Transomes/Putlogs	6-8	1
Ties	3-7	4
Guarding eg guardrails, toeboards etc	2-8	4
Loading	4-7	3
Construction Quality	2-7	3

APPENDIX D

An example of how the time element in scaffolding work could be used to help build a categorisation for a data store:-

General description of the various time periods

Erection.   Use.   Dismantling.   Store.

These can then be subdivided into smaller elements such as these.

Delivery.	Use.	Dismantle.	Receive.
Sorting.	Adapt.	Sort.	Sort.
Construction.	Maintain .	Remove.	Refurbish.
Handover.	Inspect.		Store.

By following this process of breaking down activities into their constituent parts it could be possible to discover the smallest constituent that significantly affects risk and help to indicate where the design effort should be concentrated to obtain the greatest effect.

Applying Innovation to Minimise Financial and Safety Risks

K Ridgway, A Todd and A J Wilday,   University of Sheffield

INTRODUCTION

The aim of the research project is to develop a design methodology which is based on the principles of risk assessment and uses these techniques at each stage in the design process. The paper will argue that risk assessment techniques at each stage in the design process. The paper will argue that risk assessment techniques could be applied at both the specification development and conceptual design stages to identify out of step performance and aid the innovation process. The basic hypothesis is that identifying out of step performance and conflict early in the design process causes a divergence of ideas and increases the level of innovation.

Risk assessment involves three phrases: identification of hazard, evaluation and risk and development of measures to control the risk. The paper uses the development of a typical product to demonstrate that reference to these three phrases is equally justified during the development of the product specification and the conceptual embodiment and detailed design phases.

The paper will also argue that in recent years the design process has changed significantly and it is no longer sufficient to consider the end point in the design process as the development of a product which meets the customers immediate requirements. Environmental and product liability legislation implies that it is necessary for the designer to consider the life cycle of the product and evaluate such factors as life cycle costs, maintainability, use, misuse, safety and final disposal. These factors are not considered in the traditional design methodologies unless specifically mentioned in the product design specification.

DESIGN METHODOLOGY

Pahl and Beitz (1988) carried out a comprehensive review of design methodologies before development a systematic approach to design which could be used by designers regardless of speciality.   The majority of early research into design methods concentrated on the identification and clarification of design activities and the development of 'step by step' design techniques. Kesselring (1942) developed a method of successive approximations in which he identified five basic principles of design (minimum manufacturing cost, minimum space requirement, minimum weight, minimum losses, optimum handling) which he applied to the optimisation and design of components. Niemann (1950) developed a technique which started with the definition of the task and proceeded through the development of variations to the selection of optimum solutions. Leyer (1963) suggested that design comprised three phases; development of working principles, layout and form design and implementation or detail design. Hansen (1965) was the first to develop a comprehensive design procedure comprising five phases:

Determination of task
Combination of elements to determine all possible solutions

Determination of the shortcomings of possible solutions and reduction of effects
Selection of the solution with fewest short comings
Production of documentation to permit practical evaluation

Later Rodenacker (1970) proposed eight phases for the design process comprising:

Clarification of the task
Establishment of logical relationships
Selection of physical relationships
Determination of constructional relationships
Validation of logical, physical and constructional relationships using calculations
Elimination of disturbing factors and errors
Completion of overall design
Review of the selected design

Pahl and Beitz (1988) used a 'step by step' systems approach to build upon the fundamental principles developed by the earlier research workers and produced their own systematic design method. This is a comprehensive method which provides a general framework for the design process. This design methodology is now well developed and tools and techniques have been identified for use during each phase. The tools and techniques recommended by Pahl and Beitz are listed in Tables 1 and 2. The methodology proposed by Pahl and Beitz is slightly different to that described by Pugh (1991). Pugh sub-divides design into six phases; market analysis, specification development, conceptual design, detail design, manufacture and sales. The main difference between the two methods is the composition of tasks carried out during the various phases.

REVIEW OF DESIGN METHODOLOGIES

An attempt to rationalise the various approaches is made in Table 3, where the various design methodologies are compared. The table demonstrates that the methodologies proposed by both Pahl and Beitz and Pugh are the most comprehensive and encompass the tasks identified by previous research workers.

Both Pahl and Beitz and Pugh appear to consider a product life cycle which starts with the perception of a need through to the development, manufacture and sale of a suitable product. Throughout they appear to concentrate on the efficiency of the design process rather than the effectiveness of the product designed. Current trends in design suggest that the design process should consider the product life cycle from the perception of need through design, manufacture and operation up to eventual decommissioning and disposal.

To evaluate possible weaknesses in current design methodologies the systematic approach proposed by Pahl and Beitz is considered in more detail.

Clarification of the Task

Pahl and Beitz start the design process with the development of a product idea. They recommend a detailed analysis of the market and Company before new product ideas are developed and products are planned. They comment that the selection of the correct product is vitally important due to the expense incurred in future development work. The importance

Table 1: Methods and Aids Used During the Conceptual Design Phase

STEPS / Methods	Product Planning	Clarification of Task	Abstraction	Establish Function/ Structures	Search for Solutions	Combine Solution Principles	Select Suitable Combinations	Firm up on Variants	Evaluate Concept Variants
Methods									
Market Analysis	•	⊠							
Specification		•	⊠						
Abstraction			•	⊠					
Black box representation			⊠	•				⊠	
Literature search	⊠	⊠			•				
Analysis of Natural Systems					•			⊠	
Analysis of known solutions		⊠		•	•				
Analysis of physical relationships				•	•	•			
Test Measurements					•	•		•	
Brainstorming	⊠				•				
Synectics					•				
Systematic study of Physical Processes					•				
Classification schemes					•				
Design catalogues					•				
Sketches									
Intuitive Improvements					•				
Selection Procedures					⊠	•		•	
Evaluation Methods				⊠	⊠	•		⊠	
Value Analysis									•

• Main Method   ⊠ Supporting Method

[Ref: Pahl and Beitz (1988)]

133

Table 2: Methods and Aids Used During the Embodiment Design Phase

STEPS / Methods	Identifying Embodiment Determining Requirements	Specify Spatial Constraints	Identify Function Carriers	Develop Prelim Layouts of FCs	Select Prelim Layout	Dev Prelim Layouts for Remaining Main FCs	Search for Solutions for Auxil FCs	Develop Details Layout for FCs	Dev Detail Layout for Auxiliary FCs	Check Refine Overall Layout	Evaluating	Preparing Definitive Layout	Check for Errors and Disturbing Factors	Prepare Prelim Parts List
Methods														
Specification	•	•								X	X			
Function Structure			•										X	
Solution Concept	•	•	•	X		X								
Solution Methods during function stage							•							
Checklist				•	X	•		•	•	•			X	X
Basic rules: simplicity, clarity, safety				•	X	•	X	•	•	X	X	X	X	X
Principles Force transmission			•	•		•	X	X						
Guidelines				X		X		•	•	X		•		•
Selection procedures					•		•							
Fault Tree Analysis										X			•	
Evaluation Methods							X				•			

• Main Method

X Supporting Method

[Ref: Pahl and Beitz (1988)]

Table 3: Comparison of Design Methodologies

Niemann (1950)	Leyer (1963)	Hansen (1965)	Rodenacker (1970)	Pahl and Beitz (1988)	Pugh (1991)
					Market Analysis
Definition of the task	Develop working principles	Determination of task	Clarification of task	**Clarification of task** Identification of constraints. Specification	**Specification formulation** Customer requirements and constraints
Development of variations	Layout and form design		Establish the logical relationships	**Conceptual design** Identify problems Search for solutions Develop concept variants Evaluate against criteria	Conceptual design Idea generation Selection of best solution
		Determine shortcomings of possible solutions and reduce effect	Determine constructional relationships		
Selection of optimum solutions		Select the solution with the fewest short comings			
			Check logical, physical and constructional relationships using calculations	**Embodiment design** Development preliminary layouts, select best Refine against criteria Optimise and complete form design. Check errors and cost effectiveness. Prepare preliminary parts list and production documents	Detail design Technical design
			Eliminate disturbing factors and errors		
	Implement detail design	Provide documentation to permit practical evaluation	Finalise the overall design	**Detail Design** Complete drawings Complete production plans Check all documents Document	Manufacture Design for manufacture Design for assembly
		Review the selected design			Selling and distribution

of making the right decision at the product initiation stage is demonstrated by Pessemier (1966) who produced a graph indicating the percentage of initial proposals which eventually became commercial propositions.

The graph demonstrates the considerable risk involved in the initial decision to develop a new product idea. This is supported by Wind (1982) who uses risk analysis techniques to evaluate the decision to develop a new product. Wind suggests that there are two dimensions to consider when determining the economic viability of new ideas and products.

(i) Expected return including expected costs, revenues, profits over the expected product life cycle, tax considerations and the effect on existing products.

(ii) Uncertainties in the expected costs and returns due to inflation, customer preference, material shortages, environmental conditions and competition.

The uncertainties are classed as risk where risk is defined as the variance in the rate of return.

Greenley and Bayus (1994) consider product launch and the equally difficult product elimination decisions. They point out that there is a major deficiency in the tools and techniques available to assist management in making important product launch and elimination decisions. They also point out that the majority of decisions involve some form of risk analysis.

When the risk of product failure is examined it is surprising that more time and effort is not expended in the early stages of design. Sharpe (1991) makes an interesting comparison

Figure 1: Survival Time for 100 new product proposals*

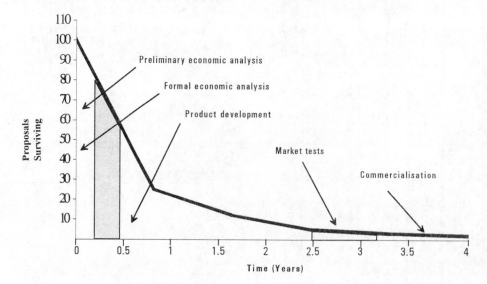

*Adapted from Pessemier (1966)

between design methods in Britain, the USA and Japan. In Britain and the USA product definition accounts for 17% of design time, design accounts for 33% and redesign for 50% of the time expended. In Japan the corresponding figures are 66%, 24% and 10% respectively. The Japanese approach can significantly reduce the cost of product development as the effective cost of making design changes increases logarithmically as the design process progresses (Parsaei et al, 1993).

As an example it is useful to consider the case of a portable magnetic based drill unit used for drilling holes in structural steelwork. Originally the Company involved manufactured a larger portable magnetic based machine for use in the construction industry. The product sold well and was a market leader. Preliminary market research indicated that a market existed for a smaller, lighter and less powerful unit which could be sold into the tool hire market. The Company realised that they could lose sales of the larger machine if existing customers, in the construction industry, preferred the smaller, lighter and less costly version. The Company based the decision to develop the new unit on intuitive judgement which incorporated years of product and market knowledge. The decision to develop the new product could have been based on the concepts of risk management as described by Flanagan and Norman (1993). The Company were successful because they had access to product and market experience if this had not been available the more formal risk management route could have been applied.

At the specification stage risk assessment will focus on the potential hazards of the functions required in the specification. At this stage, all that will be possible is a partial hazard identification where the hazards inherent in the desired functions can be found (eg cutting, impact resulting from movement, electrical shock etc). No information about the consequence or frequency can be generated at this stage because these depend on the way in which the design implements the required functions. Some products may have no inherent hazards.

Using the portable drill unit (plate 1) as an example several inherent risks can be identified at the specification stage. The machine must develop the power to remove material from the workpiece. The machine must also, by definition, by used safely in high and difficult locations and must be capable of secure attachment to the workpiece (structural steelwork). The use of power and force and the need to operate in hazardous locations provides the inherent risks.

Conceptual Design

In the first phase of conceptual design the designer abstracts the essential aims and functions of the product under consideration. When this has been achieved a number of techniques are used to generate possible solutions and examine variants. Typical techniques are listed in Table 1, taken from Pahl and Beitz. It is interesting to note that no reference is made to risk assessment techniques although some may be usefully applied as shown in Table 4.

At the conceptual design stage, different methods of implementing the required functions are explored. Risk assessment at this stage is essential if inherent safety is to be achieved in the final design. Hazard identification can be carried out on each concept. Comparison of the hazards generated with those identified during the specification stage study will indicate whether any of the concepts considered introduce hazards which are not inherent in the required functions of the product. Some approximate qualitative assessment of the likely frequency and consequence of each hazard can also be carried out at this stage and the relative risks of the design concepts can be compared. Risk assessment is more valid for comparing

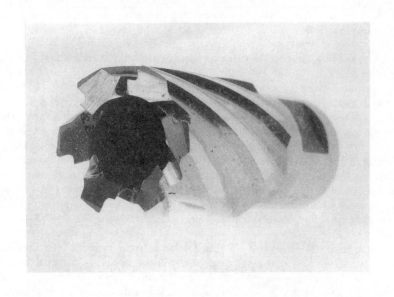

Plate 1. Portable magnetic based drill

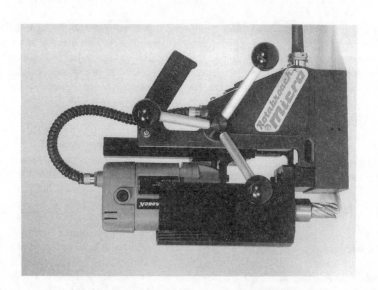

Plate 2. Annulus cutter

Table 4: Application of Risk Assessment Techniques to the Design Process

Technique	Purpose	Design Stage	Application
Hazard and Operability study (HAZOP)	Hazard identification	Detail	Assess safety of detailed design
Pre-HAZOP	Hazard identification	Conceptual	Identification of possible causes of major events
Fault Tree Analysis (FTA)	Predicting hazard frequency	Embodiment	Identification of contributing factors and quantitative assessment of risk
Event Tree Analysis	Consequence analysis and frequency prediction	Embodiment	Used to identify the factors which contribute to a hazard
Preliminary Hazard and Consequence Analysis	Hazard and consequence analysis	Conceptual	Qualitative analysis of contributing factors
Quantified Risk Assessment (QRA)	Frequency and consequence prediction	Embodiment	Requires detailed failure data
Short Cut Risk Assessment	Frequency and consequence prediction	Conceptual	Uses Qualitative assessment to produce quantified results
Concept Hazard Assessment	Hazard identification	Conceptual	Identification of relevant standards to aid safe design
Critical Examination	Hazard identification	Conceptual	Preliminary examination of design
Check lists	Hazard identification	Conceptual Embodiment	Check against list of possible hazards
Standards	Hazard identification	Specification Embodiment	Comparison with known safety standards
Sneak Analysis	Hazard identification	Conceptual Embodiment	Examines connection of components
Task Analysis	Hazard identification	Concept Embodiment	Examines operational problems
Action Error Analysis (AEE)	Hazard identification	Embodiment	Aims to reduce operator error
Human Reliability Analysis (HRA)	Frequency prediction of human error	Embodiment	Human error analysis
What if? Analysis	Hazard identification	Concept Embodiment	Asks questions pertinent to the design
Reliability Block Diagram (RBD)	Hazard identification	Embodiment	Designs safety related control systems
Failure Mode and Effect Analysis (FMEA)	Hazard identification and consequence analysis	Embodiment	Examines all failure modes and their effect
Maintenance Analysis	Hazard identification and frequency prediction for maintenance activities	Embodiment Detail	Examination of main-tenance requirements for safe operation
Structured Reliability Analysis	Hazard identification and consequence assessment	Embodiment	Examines structural failure
Method Organised Systematic Analysis of Risks (MOSAR)	Hazard identification, frequency and consequence prediction	Embodiment	Uses a series of steps to assess safety
Goal Orientated Failure Analysis	Hazard identification	Concept	Identifies factors leading to realisation of hazard
Control and Operability Study (COOP)	Hazard identification	Specification Concept Embodiment	
Fuzzy sets and Fuzzy logic	Quantification of frequencies and consequences	Embodiment	Quantifies qualitative opinions
DEFI Method	Reliability assessment	Prototype	Assess reliability of hardware
Delphi Technique	Frequency and consequence prediction	Embodiment	Translates predictions into quantifiable terms

alternative designs that attempting to prove the acceptability of a design against an objective criteria. Many of the assumptions which increase the risk during the assessment will be common in different design alternatives being compared. Risk assessment at the concept design stage will focus attention on any serious safety problems. This is very likely to cause a search for solutions to those problems and hence generate new and innovative design concepts.

Using the portable drill unit (plate 1) as an example the main functions can be identified as:

(i) Producing a hole in the workpiece
(ii) Attachment to the workpiece

Several methods of producing holes can be identified including punching, drilling, burning and erosion and electro chemical techniques. Burning is unlikely to produce holes of sufficient accuracy. Erosion and electro chemical techniques are unsuitable for isolated locations. Punching and drilling could both be used to produce holes of the required diameter. Punching produces a potential hazard due to the sudden release of energy and drilling presents a potential hazard of rotating parts.

Several methods of attaching the drill to the workpiece are available including manual clamping, vacuum and magnetic techniques. Clamping is difficult and relatively slow to use in isolated locations. Vacuum systems are feasible but there is a risk of detachment if the vacuum is lost. Permanent magnets can be used but they have limited holding power. Electro magnets have sufficient holding power but they will fail if the electrical supply is interrupted. Electro permanent magnets which only require power to magnetise and demagnetise offer an ideal solution but they are relatively expensive to manufacture. Detailed analysis of the concepts indicates that electromagnets offer the best solution.

Risk assessment can be applied to identify potential hazards and possible methods of eliminating them. For example in the design considered one potential hazard concerns the detachment of the drill from the workpiece. This could be caused by loss of electrical power or excessive axial force on the drill lifting the magnet from the workpiece. The problem of loss of power could be solved by using electro-permanent magnets. Annulus drilling, using an annulus cutter (plate 2), reduces the axial force on the drill and thus the risk of detachment. This risk can also be reduced by providing a back up clamp or holding strap.

Embodiment and Detailed Design Stages

'The embodiment and detailed design phases involve the technical design of the product and detailed design of components. Risk assessment techniques are usually recommended during the embodiment design phase as shown in table 2. During this phase hazard identification can again reveal any new hazards introduced during the conceptual design phase. The greater the detail in the design the greater the level of risk assessment possible. From the embodiment design stage onwards the risk assessment will include a consideration of risk control measures.
  All the hazards inherent in the initial product specification will require control since they cannot be eliminated. An example of such control is the guarding of rotating components, as shown in plate 1, and the use of a strap to guard against the effects of detachment of the magnet.

Standards may help in deciding how to implement hazard control and determine the level of reliability and integrity required. Innovative designs may suffer from the unavailability of the appropriate standards as there will always be a time lag before standards are developed. Risk assessment then becomes essential in deciding the adequacy or otherwise of the proposed control measures. At the detailed design stage, quantification of frequency and consequences should be possible, together with he quantification of the effect of the hazard control systems on the frequency and/or consequences.

CONCLUSIONS

Traditional design methodologies as described by Pahl and Beitz and Pugh consider the development of a product from concept through to manufacture. Both describe the design process as starting with information gathering and the formulation of a product design specification. This is followed by a conceptual design phase where ideas and possible solutions to the product design specification are developed and evaluated. The next phases involve the technical design of the product and detailed design of components. During these phases the designer considers such factors as design for manufacture and the ergonomics and aesthetics of the design. The designer may also evaluate the safety of the design and carry out some form of risk assessment. It is also clear that the existing design methodologies do not consider the extended product life cycle which starts with the initial business risks at product conception and ends with dismantling and disposal.

The review of design methodologies indicates that risk assessment is generally applied in the later stages in the design process. Unfortunately risk assessment applied at this stage has little impact on the design concept. Problems can only be addresses through small design changes or the addition of alarms and guards.

A comparison with Japanese design methodologies indicates that more time should be spent on the initial definition of the product and the development of the product design specification. Risk is an important factor in the decision to develop a product to meet a potential market need. It is clear that risk assessment, in its most basic form, can be applied in the early stages of design to identify possible hazards and assist in the development of the specification. It can also be used to assist managers in making the critical product development decisions and to clarify the aims and performance requirements of the product. The identification of hazards at an early stage assists the designer to develop innovative solutions. The case study design discussed demonstrates that the hazards can be identified and most effectively dealt with at the clarification of task stage.

Table 4 considers the application of a wide range of risk assessment techniques throughout the design process. Although these techniques are very useful the basic principles of risk assessment, ie. hazard identification, evaluation of risk and development of methods to reduce or control the risk may provide the most appropriate guideline to apply throughout the design process. By assisting the designer to clarify the aims and their consequences at the earliest stage of the design process "Engineering Consequence Design" aims to improve the design process by highlighting areas where valuable design time could be committed to greatest benefit.

REFERENCES

Flanagan R and Norman G, (1993), "Risk Assessment and Construction", Blackball Scientific Publications, UK.

Greenley G E and Bayus B L, (1994), "A Comparative Study of Product Launch and Elimination Decisions in UK and US Companies", European Journal of Marketing, Vol 28 No. 2 pp 5-29, MCB University Press, UK.

Hansen F, 1974, Konstrucktionswissenschaft - Grundlagen und Methoden, Munich, Vienna: Hanser.

Kesselring F, (1942), Die starke Konstruction, Z. VDI 86, 321-330, 749-752.

Leyer A, 1963-1971. Maschinenkonstruktionslehre, Vols 1-6 Technia-series. Basel, Stuttgart: Birkhauser.

Niemann G, 1950. Maschinenelemente, Vol 1 Berlin: Gottingen, Heidelberg: Springer (2nd ed 1965, 3rd ed with M Hirt, 1975).

Pahl G and Beitz W, (1988), Engineering Design a systematic approach, Edited by K Wallace, The Design Council, London, UK.

Parsai H R and Sullivan W G (1993), Editors, Concurrent Engineering, Contemporary Issues and Modern Design Tools, Chapman and Hall, UK.

Pessemier E (1966), New Product Decisions, McGraw Hill, New York.

Pugh S (1991), Total Design, Addison Wesley Publishing Company, UK.

Sharpe C, (1991) "Fresh Approach Reduces Product Time to Market", Design Engineering, 2, pp 26-28, UK.

Wind Y J (1982), Product Policy: Concepts, Methods and Strategy, Addison Wesley Publishing Company, UK.

Life Cycle Cost Management: a client's view

K Owen, BAA plc

INTRODUCTION

Life Cycle Cost Management (LCCM) within BAA plc is still in its embryonic stage of implementation following identification of a strategic requirement by BAA's Management Committee headed by Sir John Egan in December 1993. A Head of Life Cycle Management was appointed in early 1994 to develop a vision, methodology and implementation plan for the whole BAA group.

LCCM is extremely important to BAA, its staff, business partners and customers to enable us to provide value for money from our facilities (as owner occupiers and property developers) and to provide added value to everyone.

This paper gives a synopsis of LCCM within BAA and details major matters and key issues which need to be considered when preparing a methodology for an organisation prior to adopting a LCCM approach.

BAA's LCCM PHILOSOPHY

LCCM is a process which can ensure the achievement of our corporate strategy relating to projects (future assets). This strategy identifies the need for projects to be:-

✓   cost effective over the whole life of the asset.

✓   to world's best standards by minimising both capital and operating costs wherever feasible, without compromising safety, environment, energy, quality, operational and maintenance requirements.

BAA's definition of LCCM is 'It's BAA's structured approach to the systematic analysis of its projects (cost and performance) on a whole life basis'.

THE LCCM VISION - Diagram 1

The vision is for LCCM to be linked closely and be an integral part of BAA's Project Process, from project inception through to disposal of a facility as a 'closed loop' learning iterative process, feeding back and forwards on a continuously improving basis.

BAA has a continuous improvement culture throughout the group. It is currently spending around £1.0 million per day on projects and it is imperative that these future assets are produced cost effectively and operationally efficient.

Risk Management is inherent in this project process from inception stage onwards on all projects.

The LCCM process provides a structured approach to the analysis of projects, both for existing and proposed facilities. It assists in ensuring that decisions are subject to careful consideration and that alternative options are fully explored.

The LCCM process (see Diagram 4 herein) is linked, but not limited, to BAA's already successful Value Management/Value Engineering/Post Project and Occupancy Evaluation (VM/VE/PPE/POE) processes.

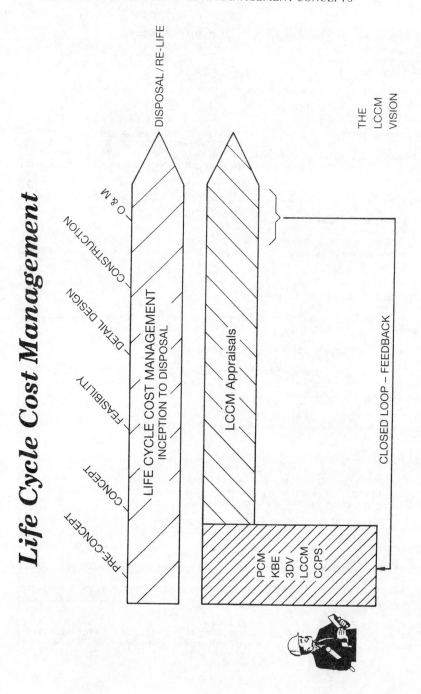

Life Cycle Cost Management

PRE-CONCEPT — CONCEPT — FEASIBILITY — DETAIL DESIGN — CONSTRUCTION — O & M — DISPOSAL / RE-LIFE

LIFE CYCLE COST MANAGEMENT
INCEPTION TO DISPOSAL

LCCM Appraisals

THE
LCCM
VISION

CLOSED LOOP — FEEDBACK

PCM
KBE
3DV
LCCM
CCPS

Diagram 1

At the VM1 study, the VM team will decide if Life Cycle Cost (LCC) is a 'key' attribute to the success of a project and if it is, the VM team will recommend its implementation to the Project Board (The Project Owners). The linked process enables operators, maintainers and end users to be involved in the decision making throughout the life of a facility.

DELIVERABLES & BENEFITS – Diagrams 2 & 3

These diagrams identify the 'key' LCCM Vision deliverables and benefits which BAA aims to achieve.

BAA's LCCM VISION – DELIVERABLES & BENEFITS		
Project Process Stage/s	Deliverables	Benefits
Inception/Pre-Concept/Concept Stages	Cost Targets - capital and operating & maintenance costs	Working with fewer Suppliers (Consultants and Contractors) focused on driving out unnecessary costs to provide realistic cost targets for BAA's business.
	Greater value for money	Cost targets will be used to produce greater value for money. This results through not setting capital cost targets unless essential for the business, which are detrimental or fail to take cognizance of on-going operational costs which are extremely important to BAA and its business partners and customers.
	In the longer term, generically model facilities	Utilise Knowledge Based Engineering (KBE) linked with 3DV (Three Dimensional Visualisation), PCM (Pro-active Cost Modelling) and CCPS (Construction Cost Planning System) incorporating LCCM to produce optimum business/facility solutions.
	Adjust generic model based on actual data	Utilising data structuring to measure the cost and performance of the operating facility against the generic model and adjust as necessary.

BAA's LCCM VISION – DELIVERABLES & BENEFITS		
Project Process Stage/s	Deliverables	Benefits
Inception/Pre-Concept/Concept Stages (Continued)	Lower total life costs	Capital cost of a new terminal building represents only 20% of its total costs over a 25 year life, as BAA operates 24 hours/day, 365 days/year. Our potential for Value for Money and cost savings (time is also money) is, therefore, enormous when focused on total life.
	More effective facilities management	LCCM can provide a life cycle plan for the chosen design option/project over a profiled life. This not only indicates the costs of replacing components/ assemblies etc., it informs the operational and maintenance personnel (BAA and business partners) of when the replacement, through maintenance management, is likely to occur. The life cycle plan, therefore, acts as a prompt to minimise disruption and loss of income and reduction of Quality Service Monitors (QSM's) for passenger/public areas and engineering.

Diagram 2

BAA's LCCM VISION – DELIVERABLES & BENEFITS		
Project Process Stage/s	Deliverables	Benefits
Feasibility and Later Project Stages	LCCM Guidelines (3 levels):- - Project Managers' Guide - Consultants' Briefing Document - Training/User Manual	The guidelines will assist in the implementation and use of LCCM/LCC throughout BAA in a consistent manner and define:- why, when, what, who does what and how to do LCCM within BAA on a common 'like for like' basis detailing:- Time Horizons, Discount Rates, Taxation Asset Lives, Maintenance and Replacement Cycles.
	LCCM Software (Spreadsheet and Database)	Spreadsheet will incorporate BAA's discount rates and risk premia for projects and taxation formulae allowing calculations to be made on a 'like for like' basis utilising industry standard software. Spreadsheet will link with LCCM database incorporating data structures on components/assemblies etc, utilised by BAA. BAA is currently working on a 'life' book. This data will allow performance benchmarking and re-engineering processes to be enhanced.

BAA's LCCM VISION – DELIVERABLES & BENEFITS		
Project Process Stage/s	Deliverables	Benefits
Feasibility and Later Project Stages (Continued)	Link into BAA's VM/VE/Post Project Processes	Linking, but not limited to, an extremely well defined and successful process already established and operating within BAA, for BAA and its business partners.
All Design Stages Onwards	BAA Designs and Operates as an Investment NOT as a Cost	By integrating design, procurement, construction and facilities management as a seamless process. BAA utilises its 'life' design standards to procure (on an integrated approach* through framework agreements) its construction and operational requirements by getting 'closer to fewer' (Consultants and Contractors) etc., through its Vendor Qualification System.

* Based upon Performance, Safety (part of BAA's Mission Statement), Availability, Reliability and Maintainability Requirements

Diagram 3

BAA's LCCM PROCESS - Diagram 4

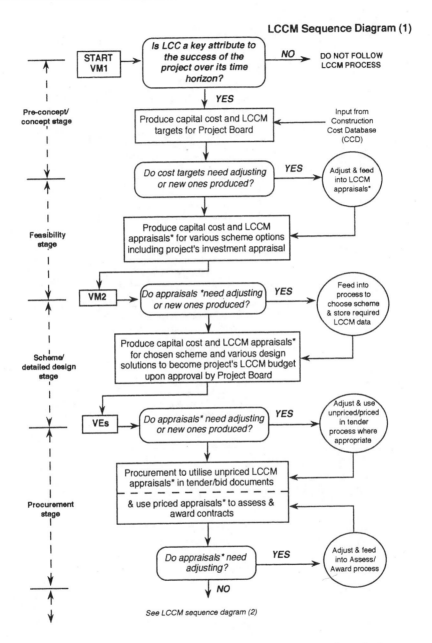

LCCM Sequence Diagram (1)

See LCCM sequence diagram (2)

Continued overleaf

BAA's LCCM PROCESS - Diagram 4 (Continued)

LCCM Sequence Diagram (2)

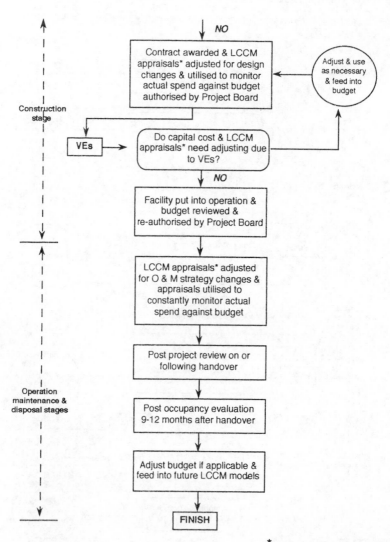

* Capital cost and LCCM appraisals will
include both capital cost & LCC targets

Step by Step

Step 1   Set the objectives of the exercise e.g. reduce running costs (operating and maintenance) costs, choose between a number of options etc.

Step 2   Identify the various options.

Step 3   Establish the period of analysis (time horizon), discount rate, inflation rate/s for the appraisal.

Step 4   Identify all the running cost items and the likely benefits associated with the options.

Step 5   Estimate the initial capital costs of the options.

Step 6   Use BAA data to calculate the occupancy periods, measure the performance characteristics, floor area, energy, use, operating and maintenance needs and cycles, cleaning costs, security, asset lives and all other likely items, based upon existing facilities' costs and performance.

Step 7   Discount future costs to present costs/values using the BAA discount rate/s.

Step 8   Make allowance in the calculations for the impact of varying inflation rates and taxation.

Step 9   Rank the options and test the sensitivity and risks of the various assumptions underlying the estimates utilising risk analysis.

LCCM EXAMPLE - Diagram 5

A simple example for the replacement of a lighting system in a retail area of an airport is as follows:-

System:	*Installation of a new energy effective lighting system*
Study Period:	*10 years*
Discount Rate (nominal):	*12.5% (inflation has been taken into account)*
Yearly energy cost:	*£1,000 per year and escalating 5% per year above the rate of inflation*
Yearly maintenance cost:	*£100*
Replacement cost of tubes at end of year 5:	*£500*
Resale value of system:	*£300 (this might only be a salvage/disposal value or may even be a cost)*

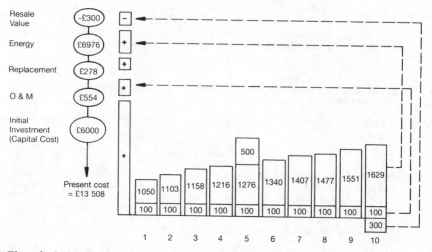

The calculation for the present cost for the replacement of a lighting system in a retail area of an airport.

Diagram 5

The basis for the appraisal is that all costs are represented in the form of a discounted cash flow in which costs are converted into present value.

LCCM PROCESS - KEY ISSUES

LCCM Appraisal Period of Analysis/Time Horizon

The LCCM appraisal time horizon is defined by its start (Year O) and its finish (Year N). Year O is selected as the first year in which expenditure occurs, which is not necessarily the current year. The selection of the LCCM appraisal time horizon (Year O to Year N) is crucial to how the completed LCCM appraisal is to be accepted by the business decision makers.

To maximise the effectiveness and realism of the LCCM appraisal short time horizons are essential. In an attempt to limit uncertainty BAA has established a maximum time horizon of 25 years using 5 year bands.

If an LCCM appraisal is to be produced for a long life asset, the Discounted Cash Flow (DCF) is to be curtailed at year 25 and a Residual Value (RV) is to be assigned to the asset in recognition of its usefulness beyond this time. The RV of an asset is its value at the end of the time horizon (Year N) on a straight line basis. The RV is to be incorporated in the discounted cash flow calculations.

When two or more alternatives with differing life expectancies are under comparison, identical LCCM appraisal time horizons must be adopted in order for the comparison to be fair.

BAA's chosen methodology is to set the study period to the shorter of the life expectancies and assign a residual value to the alternatives with the longer life expectancies.

The Discounting Process

The discount rate has two important functions. Firstly, it enables future costs over a time horizon to be brought to a present value; in effect it is an exchange rate which converts tomorrow's cost and revenues back to today.

Secondly, by converting costs which occur at both regular and irregular intervals to today it is possible to compare different options on a comparable basis ("apples" for "apples").

The method of adjusting future years' cost to allow for interest and inflation is called discounting. A pound in the future is not the same as a pound today - money has a *time value*. All future pounds are discounted (reduced in value) by applying a discount rate selected specifically for the appraisal.

Discounted present value or present costs should not be confused with real money. A new lift installation with an initial capital cost of £200,000 and a present cost of £1 million over a 25 year time horizon, taking account of all the operating and maintenance costs, does not mean that the airport has to have £1 million today to afford the £200,000 investment! However, the company needs to include relevant monies in future budgets/business plans to operate and maintain the lift.

When preparing an LCCM appraisal it is essential that all costs associated with the particular options are identified. These data may be represented in the form of a cash flow which reflects both the magnitude and timing of future expenditure.

Is It Always Necessary to Discount Future Pounds?

The need to discount future pounds depends upon the use to which the LCCM appraisal will be put. If the objective is to forecast annual costs on a year by year basis, it makes little sense to discount future pounds. However, if, on the other hand, the objective is to bring a stream of cost consequences over time to a common base in order to make some decision, then it is necessary to discount future pounds.

Inflation

"Nominal terms" v "Real terms".

There are two possible approaches to dealing with inflation. The first uses money in "nominal terms" which means that inflation predictions are built into forecasted cost and prices. The second uses "real terms" which means that all the future costs and prices are estimated at present day (real) prices, i.e. excluding inflation.

> BAA utilises "nominal" discount rates for LCCM on its projects thus taking inflation into account.

What happens when some items are likely to escalate in price faster/slower than the general rate of inflation?

Any future costs which are expected to change faster or slower than the rate of inflation, for example oil prices, should be increased or decreased by the differential cost escalation rate. The rate of inflation might change year on year for the item being considered. Future cash flows that are expected to change at rates significantly different from the general rate of inflation should be included on the basis of their actual expected costs.

Depreciation

No depreciation is provided within BAA's financial appraisals and therefore depreciation is not included within our LCCM appraisals.

Asset Lives

Judgement should be used when selecting the appropriate asset life. The standard accounting life should not be used if there are good reasons for expecting that the actual service life will be different.

Taxation

When calculating a project's life cycle costs it is important to take into account the tax implications of any expenditure as these will alter, sometimes significantly, the total life cycle costs of the project and the profitability of BAA. There are two main areas to consider. These are the capital allowances available on the project expenditure and the corporation tax impact of the revenues and costs of the project.

Plant and machinery is defined, by the Inland Revenue, as equipment used for business but not part of the fabric of the building. The allowance available on plant and machinery is 25% of the expenditure charged annually on a reducing balance basis, this is to say that 25% of the balance of expenditure is allowable each year. This is known as the *written down allowance*. Plant and machinery allowances can be claimed as and when the expenditure is incurred.

Industrial buildings expenditure also qualifies for capital allowances. These are of a different nature to those available for plant and machinery and consist of a 4% allowance given on a straight line basis, that is to say that 4% of the initial capital expenditure is deducted annually against the balance on the building. Industrial buildings allowances can only be claimed once the building becomes operational.

It is very important when calculating the life cycle costs of a project to include these allowances as they effectively reduce the overall costs of a project.

LCCM AND HOW IT WILL WORK WITHIN BAA

BAA currently owns and operates extensive facilities and is developing and constructing new facilities/refurbishments on a continuing basis (current capital spend around £1 million per day!) The airports operate 365 days a year, 24 hours a day and they are intensely used. Once a facility is put in place it will incur revenue (running costs) and the commitment is for the service life of the facility.

Revenue (running costs) consume a substantial part of the operating budget, hence it is important to balance expenditure between the capital and revenue costs. LCCM is one such initiative, where money spent today can be balanced against the ongoing cost into the future.

The use of LCCM to BAA is essential for effective decision-making in the following ways:-

- To facilitate an effective choice between alternative methods of achieving BAA's stated objectives.

- To ensure all BAA's facilities represent value for money throughout their lives, from inception to disposal.

- To identify high cost elements in BAA's operation which can be refined or eliminated to be cost effective.

- To identify the total cost commitment undertaken by BAA in the acquisition of any assets rather than merely concentrating on the initial capital costs.

LCCM identifies those areas in which revenue (running costs) might be reduced either by a change in operating practice eg hours of operation, or by changing the relevant system.

LCCM is a technique which is intended for use in decision-making, but it does not substitute for the decision-making process itself. BAA staff and consultants should use the technique to allow varying solutions to be considered.

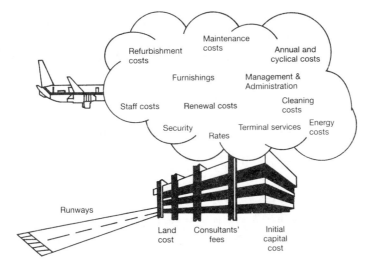

The technique can be used in four ways:-

- To help provide a basis to make a choice between two or more competing options.

- To asses the economic consequences of a given set of decisions already made.

- To provide an indication of the level of future costs (life cycle plan) likely to be incurred on a facility.

- To help focus the decision-makers', project teams', VM/VE teams' etc., minds on the future.

The technique considers only consequences which can be measured in monetary terms. LCCM embodies a quantitative approach and it makes no attempt to consider arguments which cannot be expressed in those terms.

The essence of the technique lies in looking at the economic consequences of a design decision over some period of time. It is of particular value in determining whether future monetary savings of £x justifies the initial capital expenditure of £y. It can also be used to examine a number of other kinds of decisions whose financial effects are spread over a number of years.

LCCM techniques can be applied in any area of economic decision-making but they are particularly relevant for buildings and building systems, airport facilities and infrastructure as they allow proper identification and evaluation of the risks and costs of a durable asset.

Whether a complete building, individual building element, item of plant or runway/taxiway is being considered, a decision is being made to acquire assets that are intended to last and be used over a number of years. These assets will commit BAA and its business partners not only to initial capital costs but also to subsequent revenue (running costs), day-to-day operating, security, annual and cyclical maintenance, periodic repair or replacement, cleaning and energy as applicable.

UNCERTAINTY AND RISK

LCCM appraisals involve considerable uncertainty. The most obvious point to make about the uncertainty issue is very simply that all decisions are based upon uncertain information, whether these decisions refer to estimates of initial costs or estimates of future costs. All that changes is the degree of uncertainty. More importantly, techniques now exist that allow uncertainty to be used in order to improve decisions.

LCCM appraisal techniques can be used in conjunction with risk analysis techniques (ie what if the discount rate was to change from 12.5% to 7% to 4% - what would the effect be? What if the time horizon was 15 years or 20 years instead of 25 years?) An overriding priority of BAA is to avoid surprises. Indeed, this will often be more important than searching for the lowest cost option.

Risk analysis techniques identify the primary sources of potential surprises and identify their likely impact.

MAKING BETTER DECISIONS BY CONSIDERING ALL THE OPTIONS

Whilst a LCCM appraisal looks at the balance between the initial and future expenditures, the basic idea is that spending additional sums now may well reduce expenditures in the future. However, this rule does not always hold true. Spending more today to save in the long run can be a fallacy. Making better decisions may mean reducing both capital and long term costs. In addition, more intangible benefits may flow from increased initial expenditures, in terms of improved aesthetic quality, reduced disruption during refurbishment or planned (or panic) maintenance, or increased income generating power of the building.

Every effort should be made to give monetary value to these intangible benefits in order to include them in the LCCM appraisal.

Nevertheless, where this is not possible, they are still extremely important and should be allowed to influence the design process.

THE DATA DILEMMA - See Diagram 6

The problems of collecting and analysing data are often referred to as being a major shortcoming in using LCCM appraisals. It is true that LCCM appraisals do require data. However, BAA does collect and analyse data on the operating and maintenance costs of its facilities. This is seen as a crucial element of overall cost and facilities management.

Data identifies, in detail, major areas in which BAA incurs cost and also points to ways in which potential cost savings can be achieved.

BAA maintains databases of historic costs. Information collected is used for a variety of purposes. Whilst these data are available, it is not the intention to develop a large database of information simply for LCCM. A balance has to be struck between the cost of collecting data and the potential benefits.

The components of data collection - *Diagram 6*

BAA has commissioned a number of studies on various aspects of its systems. They cover such areas as maintenance, energy usage, environment and safety. For example, the *Construction and Maintenance Systems Study* focused upon the investment in construction and maintenance related information systems. Many elements of the "Vision" included in that study are part of LCCM namely:-

- For controlled asset and facility data to be captured at the earliest practical point in the construction and maintenance cycle and be stored in such a way to be accessible to others with an interest.

- For controlled data about existing assets and facilities to be used to assist the planning, design and development co-ordination of new assets and facilities.

- For facilities planning and asset investment decision making to be properly informed, through access to accurate and up to date information about the cost and performance in use of existing assets and facilities.

- For construction and maintenance functions and operations to be brought closer together in supporting the Corporate business, through an even more interactive approach to the management of airport assets and facilities.

USING TODAY'S DATA TO MAKE TOMORROW'S DECISIONS

There are a number of general items that must be considered when investigating the revenue costs and performance of existing facilities.

Data

- Source of data.

- Conversion of data into a meaningful and structured format (eg common coding).

- How old are the data - do they relate to one year or over a number of years, how should they be averaged if we are going to use them?

- How should the data be kept up to date?

Facilities

- Is the age of the building and the main components affecting the revenue costs?

- What performance figures are available, how much electricity, gas, water, oil has been used?

- What is the cleaning programme and how are the data recorded?

- How have the operations and maintenance been managed?

- What is the condition of the facility, when was the last condition survey undertaken and what did it show?

- How has the facility been used/abused. What are the occupancy profiles and types of activities undertaken?

- What is the superficial floor areas and functional breakdown of the space used?

- What is the future life expectancy/obsolescence/decay in materials and components?

- What are the forecasts for planned and preventative and unplanned or corrective maintenance?

- What are the strategies and forecasts about modernisation, refurbishment, adaption or retrofit in future?

- What is the company's policy on recyclability and sustainability of materials, components upon disposal of a facility or part thereof?

- How has the building and parts of the building been depreciated in the company accounts for balance sheet purposes?

- How has taxation been handled?

As the list illustrates, there is a need for continually improving management of the revenue costs and performance data gathered from facilities, together with improving forecasts of future events.

BAA's LCCM IMPLEMENTATION

Pilot Studies

BAA, over the past several months, has conducted several 'pilot' studies on a LCCM basis. Some of the projects involved were:-

- Heathrow   - 100% Hold Baggage Screening - all BAA Terminals (lead by Heathrow Co-ordinator)
  - T1 Arrivals
  - Cargo Tunnel Refurbishment
  - T3 South Office Block

- Gatwick   - Office Park (Lynton - 'World Class' Speculative Development)
  - South Terminal Arrivals Baggage Scheme

- Edinburgh   - Terminal Building Eastern Extension.

LCCM has focused on real issues. In the case of the first project above, these issues, in order of significance, were as follows:-

> Firstly, operational staffing and maintenance
> Secondly, screening equipment
> Thirdly, baggage handling equipment *

* This was not as significant as we first expected it to be.

The LCCM study recommended:-

✓ where possible install a central screening facility even at the expense of additional baggage handling equipment to:-

1   reduce the number of screening machines
2   make more effective use of staff
3   reduce maintenance costs

✓ do not over provide screening equipment prior to 2001 as machines installed in 1996 will be life expired. Provide sufficient machines to achieve 'World Class' security and for March 1997 passenger numbers and add further machines (space and access safeguarded now) to suit passenger numbers growth and the fact that new enhanced technology may be available in three year's time!

✓ the LCCM study was conducted on a 6/8/10 and 12 man operating basis for 100% Hold Baggage Screening across the whole of BAA.

BAA Data Collection Structures - Diagrams 7, 8 & 9

The LCCM team within BAA have identified the 'macro' cost and data requirement areas and these are indicated on the following diagrams 7, 8 & 9:-

Diagram 7 -   details the cost categories and macro cost areas as well as maintenance types.

LIFE CYCLE COST MANAGEMENT
Example of Data Collection Structure

Maintenance (1)

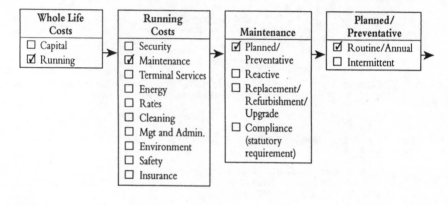

Diagram 7

LIFE CYCLE COST MANAGEMENT
Example of Data Collection Structure

Maintenance (2)

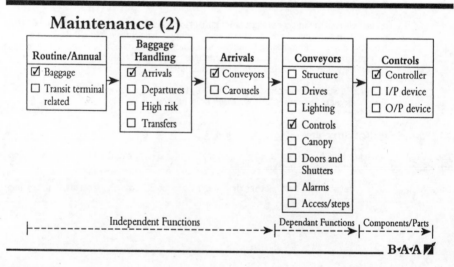

Diagram 8

Example of Data Collection Structure

Maintenance (3)

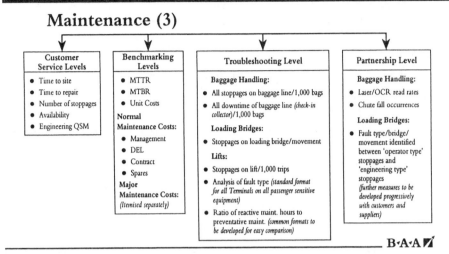

Customer Service Levels	Benchmarking Levels	Troubleshooting Level	Partnership Level
• Time to site • Time to repair • Number of stoppages • Availability • Engineering QSM	• MTTR • MTBR • Unit Costs **Normal Maintenance Costs:** • Management • DEL • Contract • Spares **Major Maintenance Costs:** *(Itemised separately)*	**Baggage Handling:** • All stoppages on baggage line/1,000 bags • All downtime of baggage line *(check-in collector)*/1,000 bags **Loading Bridges:** • Stoppages on loading bridge/movement **Lifts:** • Stoppages on lift/1,000 trips • Analysis of fault type *(standard format for all Terminals on all passenger sensitive equipment)* • Ratio of reactive maint. hours to preventative maint. *(common formats to be developed for easy comparison)*	**Baggage Handling:** • Laser/OCR read rates • Chute fall occurrences **Loading Bridges:** • Fault type/bridge/movement identified between 'operator type' stoppages and 'engineering type' stoppages *(further measures to be developed progressively with customers and suppliers)*

B·A·A

Diagram 9

Gatwick North Terminal - EXAMPLE

Total annual cost per square metre (£/m²) - Gross Floor Area

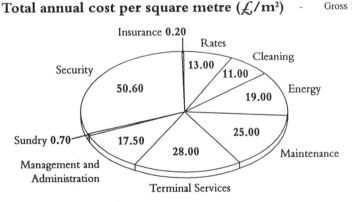

B·A·A

Diagram 10

159

Diagram 8 - details functions and components/parts as follows:-

Independent Functions

These functions stand alone as separate systems.

Dependent Functions

These functions are directly related to an independent function.

Components/parts etc. This is each component or part thereof. In the diagram we make reference to a conveyor controller, note that (I/P = Input and O/P = Output).

Diagram 9 - details four levels being; Customer Service, Benchmarking, Troubleshooting and Partnership (with suppliers).

Customer Service Levels - note that (QSM) means Quality Service Monitor.

Benchmarking Levels abbreviations are:-

- MTTR	–	Mean Time to Repair
- MTBR	–	Mean Time Between Repairs
- DEL	–	Directly Employed Labour

Partnership Levels - abbreviation OCR means Optical Character Recognition by reading baggage labels.

Top 5 faults have been identified across whole BAA group.

LCCM Business Cost Data - Diagram 10

The pie chart (*Diagram 10*) indicates the operational (running) cost drivers for BAA. The example total <u>revenue</u> annual costs have been converted to metres squared gross floor areas rates for the cost drivers.

A 10% saving on targeting energy is to be commended and is extremely important as part of BAA's environmental, energy and continuous improvement policies, however in the example, the main cost driver is Security where a 10% saving through operational efficiencies (spatial as well as cost) without compromising safety and security, would result in £5/m²/pa!

The LCCM team have charts for BAA's recent <u>new</u> terminals eg Heathrow T4, Gatwick North Terminal and Stansted (since they opened) as well as annual revenue costs per passenger.

The team also has data on other BAA Terminals.

BAA plc together with Rolls Royce MAEL Limited, Thames Water Utilities Limited, Jaguar Cars and Tesco Stores Limited have been active partners in an LCC Cross Industry Study undertaken by The University of Reading.

BAA would like to thank its partners for sharing their expertise and data within the study.

CONCLUSION

BAA hopes you will find this paper of interest and has welcomed the opportunity of presenting it to you.

The use of LCCM within BAA, we know, will have the following benefits:-

- ✓ a more effective and informed approach for data presentation to BAA's decision takers.

- ✓ a basis for predicting future running and replacement costs and when they occur.

- ✓ a management tool to ensure that a facility is being used effectively and maximum value for money is being obtained and documented.

- ✓ an aid in identifying and assisting in the balancing of future expenditure of an asset.

- ✓ an aid to benchmarking for the future.

- ✓ focused on the macro costs for our business.

WAY FORWARD

Finally, this paper presents a concept which BAA is working on to bring to fruition. For LCCM to be a success throughout the UK Construction Industry we need to work towards the production of a LCCM standard which will form an integral part of tendering procedures throughout the industry. It is hoped this LCCM paper will stimulate creative ideas and create the impetus to produce a LCCM standard for the UK Construction Industry. The author would like to hear from interested parties and can be contacted at BAA on 01293 595469.

REFERENCES:-

BAA thanks Malcolm James of the Health & Safety Executive for inviting us to present this LCCM paper.

BAA acknowledges the University of Reading Department of Construction Management and Engineering for their assistance in the production of LCCM within BAA to date, namely, Professor Roger Flanagan, Naomi Garnett, Lee Fanning and Carol Jewell, all with the support of Professor Norman Fisher.

The author would like to thank BAA and its Directors for their support in driving this subject forward and finally, thanks to my Secretary, Louise, for all her hard work in putting the paper in print.

SESSION 3 : The Discussion

J.Mather	Feasibility study on techniques for data collection to support risk assessment in civil, mechanical and structural engineering.
M.James	Factors affecting safety cost and quality of scaffolding.
Professor K Ridgeway	Applying innovation to minimise financial and safety risks
Keith Owen	Life cycle cost management (LCM) : a client's view (BAA plc)

Pam Waldron, HSE.

I am concerned here that there is a risk that we have not yet addressed, that is the risk of going overboard and making it far too complicated. I have to say that the accidents which pass my desk and the desks of my colleagues everyday have a boring predictability about them. They are in the main very simple, the three Fs. People fall off, people fall into and things fall on people. There are very few incidents where there is actually a very complicated risk that has not been dealt with. My view is that the industry is very good at those sort of risks by and large and should commend itself that it is good at those sort of risks. It is the others which we are not addressing and which I feel we need to put our effort into. Bear in mind also that there is a conservative estimate of 40% under reporting of construction accidents. We think we get all the fatal accidents but are not absolutely sure.

So I would say then if we are really going to make any impact let us not get into the COSHH philosophy of going into great detail, of complicated paperwork systems, which still leave us a little uneasy about whether we are dealing with the risks on the site. HSE has a declared enforcement policy which is about proportionality. This means that you will not face formal enforcement action for pure paper offences, what we are looking for is that you address real risks.

E Hambly

May I put a question to you ? can you make any comment, a generalisation, about management's assessment of the risks in the situations you are talking about? What could they do that would make the risks less likely to happen?

Pam Waldron

There are two aspects. One which we are really here to talk about is the design phase when much can be done to design out some of the risks, that is clear and that really needs to be addressed. On the site it is very much management of risk, the designer chooses the risk and the contractor manages the residual risk. One has to bear in mind all the difficulties that the industry has, because that is what causes us to have the difficulties with the safety culture which is the transient nature of the workforce, the subcontracting which goes on and so on.

E Hambly

Can I just pick you up on that comment ? it was a thought a question, a question for John, that came up with the scaffolding. I wonder how much the QRA can take account of the very tight market place the subcontractors are working in and the sort of contract conditions that they are trying to erect scaffold by ?

J.Mather
If that is the situation, you would expect the resultant risks to increase.

Chairman
Are you able to put this into your modelling?

J.Mather
You could actually, as has been said before, consider the consequences as financial risks as well as deaths and injuries. It is possible to take account of all of these things within a risk assessment framework.

A.Maitra, HSE.
I would like to counter what was said earlier. Yes it is complicated at the start, but so is bending theory, but we end up with M/Z and that is what we are trying to achieve here. The initial research will seem complicated, it will seem difficult, it will seem unworldly, but at the end of it, when the manual is produced, it will be an easy text to follow. That is what we are trying to achieve.

Chairman
I don't think the contribution was in anyway contradictory to what you said.

M.North, AEA Technology.
In the presentations so far there has been a considerable emphasis on risk assessment rather than the overall risk management. The risk assessment is only a small part of the management process. This is also backed up by what has just been said about the detail involved in assessment. The assessment should only be in sufficient detail to fit the risk one is trying to manage. Therefore, on a fairly small contract - say, as mentioned earlier, £1 million, it may not be necessary to start looking in detail at quantitative assessment. A more qualitative assessment may be all that is required.

E Hambly
A comment that was made to me at lunch about the small contracts was that the regulations, the codes and the standards have all been developed to cover routine situations. Therefore, if you keep to them, you have done most your risk assessment and management in the context of that.

M.North
That is the point. For a small contract, you simply cannot afford to do a full quantitative risk asessment of the form that has been put forward in some of the presentations.

A.Shiner, Kone Lifts Ltd.
The views I am going to express are mine not my company's. I think you have hit the nail on the head for the reason for the existence of theCDM regulations.

A couple of years ago I went to a meeting in Huddersfield where they were first introduced to the industry. I was shocked at the reaction of certain parts of the industry. The view that I have of the regulations is that they are there to promote good engineering practice and safety. That implies that any contractor and subcontractor should have the time and resources to do the work properly. Does the HSE agree with that?.

M.James, HSE.
I am quite sure that the HSE would agree with you most wholeheartedly and of course the CDM regulations require that resources are provided for safety considerations. I think one of the interesting things about the CDM regulations is the stress that is put on the duties of the client and the designer that have not been apparent before. The stress on the designer's duty is one of the spurs for the type of work that I am doing.

E Hambly
Would it be possible for the last questioner to describe the type of situation where the time available is not sufficient? Give us an example.

A.Shiner
We get situations where a building is being constructed and a brand new lift may be required; to be delivered and installed inside eight weeks. Our lead time from our factories is eight to nine weeks and we walk away from such requests. But how many smaller companies or companies with turnover difficulties don't ?

E Hambly
What proportion of your orders/requests do you find yourself in such a situation?

A.Shiner
Presently I would say 50% of requests are what I would term short time. But they shouldn't be, if the construction is being properly planned in the first place.

M.James
It is one of the reasons for doing a risk assessment, the whole area of risk has got to be tackled. I presume in trying to meet those tight deadlines that someone somewhere is paying money that doesn't need to be paid. If such waste can be identified and made part of the contract, then the client is going to be encouraged to get the optimum arrangement that I was talking about.

A Shiner
Indeed, one of the areas at the moment where there is a lot of short time ordering going on is the modernisation of lift equipment. Basically, with our factories, we can do this on the odd special occasion because there is sufficient slack in the system. However, if everyone begins to play that game, all that happens is that the prices simply go up. It simply introduces inefficiency.

P.Godfrey, Sir William Halcrow and partners.
First of all, I agree entirely that what we are talking about is the basic engineering process. In all that we are talking about, we are returning to the original concepts as to what engineering was about. I was trying to make the point that it is about satisfying what people need, not just about fulfilling some code of practice. The point that I wanted to make, and it was generated

by the earlier discussions and the Chairman's earlier remark as to where we had seen benefits from these processes, was that we'd been employing the systematic approaches to risk assessment and, more recently, to value management. In the last three or four years we have had fees in the order of £5M - £10M from that type of work. I can categorically say that we have saved our clients more money than it has cost them.

I can say that, on occasions, we have removed various safety provisions that were in the plan and committed in the plan, by demonstrating that they were ineffective and not doing their job properly. That, clearly, is money in the bank.

I wanted to put this as an example to counter ' let's keep it simple', which, incidentally, I normally agree with. But what I am saying is that there is a great deal of benefit to be had from thinking about the issues properly and consider that this is a basic process of design.

M.James
There has been a study done in the EEC concerning the best time to deal with the risk. I'm talking about construction now, but it would apply right across the board, particularly in the area that Keith has been talking about. This suggested that something approaching 95% of the problems that occur in the build stage could have been eliminated at the design stage. When the cost implications of that are considered they are truly enormous. This in itself justifies the attempt to throw all of the risk analysis into the design stage even though it might be a little more complicated.

K.Ridgway, University of Sheffield.
I don't think the example of the drill showed it but, really, the risk never changed. Although it was dealt with right at the detailed design stage, in the traditional design sense it was always there right from the start. We knew the risk was there at the conceptual stage and it can be designed out then. That is one of the main points we are making.

D.Blockley
I would just like to reinforce this discussion by pointing out that what I really think is happening is the coming together of management thinking and design thinking. I'm interested in the parallels between how managers go about their job and how engineers go about theirs. Both are making decisions, both are managing people and both are managing artefacts. If you interpret the quality idea in a very general sense, the only difference is that engineers are using scientific modelling, are using technological modelling - a firmer type of knowledge, if you like, than the general management uses. However, you can see that the principles of designing and engineering things are very very close to quality management in the general sense. We have got the opportunity of bringing these together in one methodology. I think that is what the academics amongst us ought to be trying to develop more.

E Hambly
If you look at the motor car in the last twenty years, it has had enormous improvements in performance and safety designed into it. If one were to say that if the designers right at the beginning could have really thought about it we could have had it 100 years ago. We are learning all of the time and there is a limit as to how fast we can actually improve.

D.Blockley

Everyone is learning all of the time. There is nothing novel about that whether it is management or engineering.

E Hambly

I'm sceptical about how much thinking can go into each stage of development.

K.Ridgway

I think the inherent risk was always there in the motor car. We always had the speed problem. We had the power problem. We could have probably seen early on that a seat belt would have been of benefit, there was always protection built into the car. Later on we've learnt more about damage and damage assessment and we've improved that, but the risk was always there.

E Hambly

It is important to recognise that you cannot always make enormous strides forward.

E Hambly [to K Owen]

Earlier on you threw out two figures of £100 million for capital and I thought £400 million operating.

K.Owen, BAA plc.

That is correct.

E Hambly

Was that after taking account of discount rate?

K.Owen

Yes. BAA's discount rate when we started the project off, on that basis, was initially 12.5%, which is quite high.

J.Dawson, Rendall Palmer and Tritton

How have you dealt with risk and uncertainty in your cost models?

K.Owen

As far as risk is concerned, I would go back to two presentations earlier this afternoon. It is early days with BAA. This process has been in operation for about six months, it is still embryonic. But it has been well thought through and we have to make sure it is successful.

The way we would look at the risks in terms of doing a life cycle cost, would be to pull the suppliers in, with ourselves and actually go through the matter in detail in terms of what the risks are to that particular product. If we take the screening equipment : what are the risks of that failing, very very significant, so we've had to do tests to minimise the risks. We are not talking about taking insurance policies out, yes, we have looked very carefully at what the risks are and how easily we can put another piece of equipment in there in a very short space of time.

J.Faulkner, consultant.

Something we have had today, is that risk management is something which applies across the whole spectrum of project management. In other words it is a technique which can be applied at every stage, right through from the very concept to the demolition of the job at the end. I think we should realise that and it is not just one particular aspect we should be concentrating on. It applies to the design, it applies to the construction, to safety, to cost, to planning and every aspect of the project. I would not like to go away from here thinking that this is just purely a safety question although safety is very important.

We have heard from Mr.Owen, an example of what I would term an enlightened client who obviously knows what he is doing on a project and enlightened clients always get the best jobs. I have a somewhat similar question to the previous one. Where is the risk analysis applied at these various stages ? you've spelled out all the stages, there should be presumaby not necessarily analysis but some consideration of risks at each one of these stages. I wonder what you had done on this and I suppose we are all rather interested particularly in view of unfortunate incidents which must increase the life cycle cost of Heathrow considerably. I wonder if any thought at all had been given to that happening.

K.Owen

Obviously I can't discuss Heathrow Express in terms of the findings from that. But in answer to your question on the risk analysis and risk management : that is looked at, as I believe a member of the audience said earlier, within the value management processes we have. If we have a VM study workshop then we would go through a risk management process, we would keep it simple in that we would probably score the risk on a scale of 1 - 5; then we would look at the probability of it occurring and put some weighting to it. That is the way we approach it. We don't have Monte Carlo simulations or anything of that nature. We have not gone down that route, we've kept it quite simple in our approach but that does happen at every VM study. As far as the Heathrow Express and the likelihood of happening what happened; I don't think anybody could have foreseen that. We didn't foresee the Gulf War, it just happened. But we have to manage accordingly.

E.Dore, Standing Committee on Structural Safety.

Following the previous questioners, and in relation to Mr.Owen's contribution, I am so impressed with the thoroughness of the the LCM analysis that I feel absolutely certain that, although he hardly mentioned safety, there was a consideration of risk and safety and its relevant costs in all those packages. Could I ask you on a matter of detail, have you a particular policy in procurement to safeguard BAA against the worst effects, if there are any, of design and build ?

K.Owen

BAA has produced a procurment matrix for its business which looks at all the different procurement routes. The team who go through the analysis decide for themselves which is the best route to follow. Design and build ? well if we do a baggage system that is partly design and build we don't have a problem with that. We don't simply letthe contractor go ahead and design and build what he wants to design and build, we pull him in and challenge him, we lay down the performance criteria that this baggage system has to operate under. For instance, there is a safety requirement that it has to operate under : the belt can't be more than 2 mm below the side of the skirting otherwise we are stopped and damage will occur. We want it within the defined tolerances, we want it to be reliable so it will operate 99% of its time, all the year through with no problems. That's the approach we take, even with a design and build contract. It doesn't matter who it is.

E Hambly

Do you manage to put the life cycle costs into the bid ? in other words are the suppliers penalised if there are costs later on ?

K.Owen

We haven't gone that far yet but it has been considered. We want to be in a win-win situation. So, for example, if we have an escalator manufacturer and we are tied in for five years, we ask him about the likely operating costs of this escalator and tie him to that. If it gets under that we will share the savings. If it goes over that then we may well just sit there and accept those costs for now, simply to start the process off.

A.Maitra, HSE.

Listening to all the speakers today one is left with the impression that data collection is a very important part of what we are talking about today. There is a lot of data around and if people were happy to share it we might progress more quickly than we have done to date. Has anyone on the panel any ideas how we get over 'commercial in confidence', to help us develop ECD?

E Hambly

I was talking earlier today to Adrian Ellis, Roger Evans, Mr.Dore and others. First of all, the HSE has a great deal of information and I would hope that we can find some way of you releasing it, in confidential form, to an organisation like the Standing Committee for Structural Safety, so that lessons can be learnt from information you are holding and unable to divulge in a normal way. Secondly, it has also been suggested that the Institution should have a very low cost publication similar to the Chemicals which describes case histories, near misses and so on in a way that the descriptions aren't an embarassment. We are going to have to pursue this.

A.Delves, Ove Arup.

I would like to make a general observation from the discussion that has taken place between risk assessment and the risk management. There seems not to have been enough concentration on risk management although, I did miss this morning's comments and presentations. Risk assessment is part of the process but the question of risk management is of equal, if not greater, importance. Looking at the CDM regulations it is such a good example of a basis of risk management. The fundamental thing it establishes is a plan, risk management must be like cost management and time management and any other management. Firstly, you must establish a plan against which you then monitor performance and then control and make decisions.

I think the work that Arup and partners did with the HSE and the CIC, in the early days in forming a designer's handbook for the CDM Regulations, was very valuable to both ourselves and the HSE. It identified that really the risks can be eliminated in the early stages of design and that design is a converging process. Certain things can be looked at in detail at various stages of the process and in the brief that we prepared it is mentioned. We do try and identify a plan for HSE, that is prepare a plan at each stage of the design and on that plan pass the information onto the next stage. What does CDM do? It produces a plan at the end of design and passes it on to construction, as a risk management tool. I was pleased to see, in the last presentation, a breaking down of the process. Unless we break down the process and break down the components I don't see how we can actually move forward in risk management.

S.Saggu, Sir William Halcrow and partners.
I would like to make a minor comment in relation to the interesting presentation of Mr.Owen. Decommissioning, because they are considering overall life cycle costs. It was not clear from the flow chart where it appeared, could you explain where it is ?

K.Owen
It is not hidden. It is a real cost to BAA but we don't really decommission our facilities we just relife them.

A. Shiner, Kone Lifts Ltd.
A personal opinion, a reflection, the design and build of the boom era saw lifts installed in steel framed buildings which took the slightly different view of ' build it and we will design it as we go'. Would anyone care to comment on the viability of that approach for the future with respect to the CDM regulations ?

B.Neale, HSE
The short answer, in broad policy terms, is that the regulations do not constrain the procurement options. They impose various reponsibilities on those at every stage of the procurement option, so they don't close down the options. It clearly makes meeting the duties more difficult in some cases than others but that doesn't imply a foreclosure of any particular type of option. Part of the complexity and the problem we had in making the regulations was to try and get a package of legislation that did reflect adequately all of the various types of construction procurement that was currently extant in the U.K., which isn't necessarily the case elsewhere in Europe, and design a model that was workable for everbody.
I hope we have achieved that. It may be inevitably that it is more difficiult for some than others but that is your choice, so be it.

A.Maitra
I think the important point of today's discussion, from my point of view, is the important role that engineers have to play in leading and developing risk management in the fields of mechanical, chemical, construction etc. We have a very important role to play and I believe we should all grasp it. When I saw the hands go up this afternoon in response to the Chairamn's question 'are we making it too complicated ?' I thought well if we don't do it someone else will. We are gathered here today to try and assist you to grasp the nettle and to take the lead in developing risk management. However, be warned, if we don't someone else will and we will end up further down the management ladder.

E Hambly
Is the Arup booklet essentially on the safety plan and its management or do you also look into the three F's that were mentioned earlier?

A.Delves
The booklet is basically a designer's handbook. It is to assist designers in implementing the CDM regulations, leading to their input into the health and safety plan as designers in

accordance with the requirement to work and cooperate with the planning supervisor. That is its general trend and it attempts to give designers badly needed advice on how to do that and, of course, risk assessment comes into that. It is one of the very difficult questions we had to answer, how do we incorporate that ? and what advice is given ? We have gone for the very simple approach that the HSE have recommended in the booklet. It has yet to be seen if that is satisfactory but of course for very complex projects a detailed analysis will be required.

E Hambly
Does it have catalogues of risk? Take for example this document, the code of practice, it has descriptive advice on how to go through it but I find that I am none the wiser at the end of it.

A.Delves
Remember it is a brief for a designer's handbook, not the designers handbook; this is for publishing firms to take on. We do give examples in which we identify the major reasons for accidents. We are not concerned only with accidents but with ill-health as well and I think the latter needs to be recognised in the CDM regulations.

B.Finney, Sir William Halcrow.
I am concerned that the risk assessment can be over complicated. I would like to assure people that, within Halcrow, we have tried a simpler approach. Engineers with little training coped with it very well, once they were set on the correct road. So, if you keep it simple, there is no doubt in my mind that engineers can cope with it.

P.Godfrey, Sir William Halcrow.
This question of complexity does require quite a lot of thought from the industry. I have three bullet points that may help to sort this out. Firstly, concentrate on how people behave and, therefore, concentrate on what they want, because what they want tends to guide how they behave. Secondly, focus on what is important and, thirdly, focus on the future rather than on an analysis of the past.

With those three things in mind I have seen various documents that have required us to identify all risks, all hazards and the like. That is an impossible requirement. What we have to do is to adjust our position to focus on what matters. I would like to say that any documents that have got that word 'all' in need very careful scrutiny.

M.James, HSE.
I would like to go back to where I started, the opportunities to deal with the risks that are around in engineering are far better dealt with before the actual project starts. Everything we have heard emphasises that and it would be well worth pursuing. I would like to reinforce what Patrick has just said, that whatever system is developed it has to be user friendly, it has to be something you can actually commit your resources to, where they are most needed. HSE has said in the past that it is very foolish to spend money in an unfocussed manner, it has to be focussed and the thrust over the next few years should be to develop ways of actually focussing so that the money that we do have can be spent effectively.

K.Ridgeway, University of Sheffield.
With regard to the complexity issue, risk management must be simple enough for people to use because the people at the sharp end who are using the techniques and actually designing things.

K.Owen, BAA plc.
You must have some complexity at the start of the process. The whole point of my contribution was the collection of data. However we must have a model to fit that into and that has got to be done at the early stages. When it is finally developed it should be much simpler.

E Hambly
The programme asks me to do a summary but Patrick Godfrey has largely done it for me. However, I will go over some of the points that have been made. I think this question of near misses and us having a much better understanding of the risk environment we live in by publicising the near misses, and so on, is something that has seriously to be addressed. Certainly, it would improve our group experience so that when we come to do risk assessments we actually spot the hazards.

I come back to the questions put by Adrian Ellis in the keynote address, in the context of Engineering Consequence Design. What tools can the HSE provide us with to make us at the design stage get a better visualisation of the risks and hazards that are coming along so that from the very start a risk assessment and risk management happens? Well I think the contribution about the three F's was fundamental to that. Any documents that are produced in the near future should concentrate on these types of common problems to help the majority of designers to deal with them.

In order for the CDM regulations to become widely used, they have to be understood by the majority of us. The more complex projects already have the experts deeply involved in them. It was mentioned earlier that for small projects it is not anticipated that risk assessments need be much more complicated than they are at the moment. In other words designing to the current regulations, codes and standards for routine situations is, in a way, doing a risk assessment. But we do need a series of examples of risk assessments for simple projects to satisfy CDM, and to help us identify hazards.

Earlier I referred to method statements and I think I should explain what I mean by method statements, as they take all sorts of forms. The type I had in mind were ones I saw a lot of about five years ago to do with underpinning of buildings in London. A method statement might consist of twenty pages of sketches where the first stage shows the site or the building that is to be modified and the next stage shows something taken out and something else put in. One could go through the diagrams and see the project developing and, although, the form was sketchy it had a step by step construction process, all the stages were visualised. The drawing of the temporary works or final works, where everything was drawn on top of the other, didn't actually show how it was to be done.

Returning to Patrick Godfrey's remark, you have got to think of the people doing the job, not so much the final ironmongery. This I see as being good contracting practice at the moment before any works are started. What we are now talking about, in the context of CDM, is something designers should be doing, also at the start of projects. One or two very famous collapses would not have occurred, I am sure, if the designers had done a proper method statement at the start, detailing how something was to be built. Unfortunately, method statements are largely produced for management considerations. But, in the context of today's discussion, management and safety go hand in hand therefore, having done the method statement, one can brainstorm the improvements, brainstorm the risks and brainstorm the opportunities.

We've had a whole variety of flowcharts placed before us today and personally I find those much less meaningful to me than diagrams of the ironmongery. As was said earlier, we can have systematic methods but they must not be comprehensive. We must focus on the essential parts of the problem, we must not lose the wood for the trees.

I would like to thank all of the speakers for describing all of the risk assessments they have been involved in, the risk management and life cycle costing and so on. Thank you all for your papers.

Risk management in civil, mechanical and structural engineering : an overview of the discussions

The Chairman, in summing up, highlighted a number of points. He emphasised that designing to current regulations, codes and standards for <u>routine</u> situations is equivalent to doing a RA. He drew attention to the importance of good method statements, stating : "one or two very famous collapses would not have occurred, I am sure, if the designers had done a proper method statement at the start as to how it was to be built. Method statements are largely produced for management considerations. In the context of today's discussion management and safety go hand in hand and, having of course having done the method statement one can, of course, brainstorm the improvements, brainstorm the risks and brainstorm the opportunities. As was said earlier we can have systematic methods but they must not be comprehensive. We must focus on the essential parts of the problem, we must not lose the wood for the trees".

The main points emerging from the discussions were:

Risk management related issues

1. There has been no improvement in accident statistics for 15 years despite improvements in project planning. Thus a more structured and integrated approach to hazard identification and risk control is needed.

2. All QRA must start with a qualified assessment, ie, identifying the hazards. In addition, assessments should be proportional to the risks. In some cases qualitative assessments will suffice.

3. There is no point in doing a risk assessment unless it is part of a risk management programme, which makes transparent the consequences of management action or in-action.

4. Engineering judgement should play an important part in risk management. The sensitivity of the analysis must be looked at carefully, ie, does a change in one parameter make a large difference to the outcome of the QRA.

5. If you are implementing existing standards in a quality way the risk assessment has been done for you. It is then down to management to ensure the intention is implemented.

6. Another delegate emphasised the usefulness of the HSE Guidelines on successful H&S management for ensuring a systematic approach to the setting of standards to cover the whole life cycle of a system.

7. A plea was made to focus on hazard management, rather than probabilistic risk assessment (PRA). Others disagreed as you need to assess risks to decide relative importance of hazards - hazard management and PRA are equally important. A risk assessment was seen as an essential first step to understanding the problems.

8. Success depends on quality management and an awareness that accidents and incidents and other forms of loss eat into profits, as underlined by the HSE study on 'Cost of Accidents at Work' and the increasing evidence about the relationship between safety management, quality management and profitability.

9. **Errors**, eg, sub-surface defects in materials, **may lead to design faults**, eg, overstressing of the section, **and faults may lead to failures** [see Blockley and Wigley/ discussion 2]. Risk management should create an organisation which (i) provides procedures for detecting errors (ii) assesses the impact of the error, to determine whether it could lead to a fault (iii) asseses the impact of the fault, to detrmine whether it could lead to a failure and, finally, (iv) assesses the impact of a failure, to determine what processes will minimise its effects.

10. An interesting application of RA being used to define a construction sequence, and the eventual consequences of the decisions, can be found in Walker's book on the Severn Tunnel.

11. The ability to learn from other peoples mistakes is a very valuable process in terms of management of risk. Without some understanding of failures that have occurred it is difficult to conduct a risk assessment (RA). We need to change the culture so that information on failures is systematically recorded.

12. There should be greater sharing of information on risks and risk management. The information could be annomised and presented as case histories, lessons from near misses etc. The Institution of Chemical Engineers produces a "Loss Prevention Bulletin" which includes such information. ICE should do the same.

13. (Proprietary inhibitions may be a problem?) The Standing Committee on Structural Safety is attempting to stimulate the industry and profession to report near misses that could in other circumstances have been serious accidents.

14. The importance of a positive safety culture was recognised. Business Process Re-engineering was seen as a way of changing culture for the better, and it is down to senior management to drive it.

15. It was agreed that what is needed is a change in the culture of our industry. But this is hindered by the transient nature of the workforce and the amount of subcontracting - factors which have consequences for developing positive safety cultures - cf the experience of the chemical industry [see Willday/ discussion 1].

16. In our idustry, if we stop people falling off/into and articles onto people we would make a significant dent in the accident statistics [see Waldron/discussion 3].

17. Good safety performance is inextricably linked to good company performance [see Sockton/discussion 1].

ECD Related Issues

18. The techniques for assessing health and safety risks can be used or adapted for assessing other risks. One delegate [see Milloy/discussion 1] gave an example where RA demonstrated that investment in a further system would be a total waste of money as current systems were sufficiently robust to render risks ALARP. The money could be used to make improvements elsewhere.

19. The principles of designing and manufacturing artefacts are very similar to quality management in a general sense. ECD provides an opportunity of bringing them together in one methodology.

20. About a third of our highway bridges are over 70 years old. Loads are continually increasing. Each time a load increases the inbuilt safety factor reduces - unfortunately, nobody knows what that factor is [see Leadbeater/discussion 1]. Tools to help us exercise professional judgement are needed.

21. Remember, a cheap way of managing risk today may not be so cheap in 50 years time [see Mann/discussion 1].

22. An EU study found that about 90% of the problems that occur in the build phase could have been eliminated at the design stage. We therefore need to do more risk analysis at the design stage to reap the potential benefits implicit in this statistic.

23. Looking at hazards and risk control provides opportunities to look at project scheduling, production methods etc. One delegate cited an example where this process led to a change in the entire contract strategy and increased profits by £1m to 1.5m on a £30m contract [see Brand/discussion 2].

24. Design consultants are already saving clients money by employing a systematic approach to risk assessment. Improved techniques are needed to generate further savings and encourage others to use them. We might find these complicated at first, but they can be made simpler as we gain familiarity and make them more user friendly. So keep it simple is a long term aim - not a short term one. Simplistic tools will not help organisations see major risks, eg the Heathrow Tunnel collapse. Other queried whether such an event was foreseeable (surely tunnels have collapsed before!)

25. Much can be done at the design stage to eliminate or reduce risks. Subsequently it is very much a process of risk management to 'control' the residual risks.

Points relevant to CDM Regulations

26. Method Statements and risk assessments go hand in hand. This is why the CDM Regulations premier requirement is for a clear description of a project's aims and objectives.

27. The CDM Regulations provide a good basis for risk management. First you must establish a plan against which you monitor performance and decide on further actions/controls. This plan is passed on to the constructor to manage the risks highlighted.